Peace Is This Moment

THICH NHAT HANH

Mindful Reflections for Daily Practice

PARALLAX PRESS
BERKELEY, CALIFORNIA

PARALLAX PRESS

2236B Sixth Street
Berkeley, CA 94710
parallax.org

Parallax Press is the publishing division of Plum Village
Community of Engaged Buddhism

Cover and text design by Katie Eberle

Author photograph © Plum Village Community of
Engaged Buddhism

The material in this book comes from books and articles
written by Thich Nhat Hanh and previously published by
Parallax Press.

Printed in Canada by Marquis

Library of Congress Control Number: 2023944715

1 2 3 4 5 MARQUIS 27 26 25 24 23

EDITOR'S NOTE

Wholesome seeds of mindfulness, peace, joy, and freedom are already there in each of us. In every moment, we are given an opportunity to water them.

Let each teaching in *Peace Is This Moment* fall on you like a daily dose of Dharma rain. In this way, Thich Nhat Hanh's words can water our wholesome seeds; that's the profound purpose of this book. If we give these teachings some time and space to sink in—for instance, by sitting each day with one passage and a cup of tea—we are doing enough. The flower of insight will bloom on its own.

LIGHTING THE TORCH OF AWARENESS

We lead extremely busy lives. I know people who say they don't even have enough time to eat or breathe; it appears to be true! What can we do about this? Can we take hold of time with both hands and slow it down?

First, let us light the torch of our awareness. Let us learn how to drink tea, eat, wash dishes, walk, sit, drive, and work in awareness. We don't have to be swept along by circumstances. We aren't just a leaf or a log in a rushing river. With awareness, each of our daily acts takes on a new meaning. We discover that we're more than machines, that our activities aren't just mindless repetitions. We find that life is a miracle, the universe is a miracle, and we too are a miracle.

SOMETHING WE CAN
BELIEVE IN

Mindfulness is something we can believe in. It's our
capacity simply to be aware of what is going on in the
present moment. When we drink a glass of water and
know that we're drinking a glass of water, mindfulness
is there. When we sit, walk, stand, or breathe and know
that we're sitting, walking, standing, or breathing, we
touch the seed of mindfulness in us. Mindfulness is
the kind of light that shows us the way. It's the living
buddha inside of each of us. Mindfulness gives birth to
insight, awakening, compassion, and love.

MINDFULNESS CAN
PRODUCE MIRACLES

Meditation, the practice of mindfulness, helps us to be fully present and to touch the beauty and wonders of life, the refreshing and healing elements. By appreciating these positive things, we can release negative elements easily. We don't need to practice sitting meditation for ten years to cross over to the shore of well-being; we need only a few seconds. The practice of mindfulness can produce miracles. Looking at the blue sky, we take one deep breath and touch its immensity, solidity, and freedom. This is very nourishing.

BEING IN TOUCH

We have to be in touch with the present moment, the wonderful life that is present in us and around us. The birds sing. The wind soughs in the leaves of the pine. If we're not in touch, our life is wasted. When we're in touch, we're nourished and we're transformed. Being in touch also means being in touch with the suffering—in our own body and our own person, in our environment, in our family, and in our society. Getting in touch with suffering, we'll know what we need to do to transform it.

On one hand, we need to be in touch with what is wonderful because that will nourish us. And on the other hand, we have to be in touch with our suffering so that we can understand, love, and transform.

CALL SUFFERING BY ITS
TRUE NAME

We recognize the suffering that exists inside of us and around us. Our practice isn't to get away from our real problems, difficulties, and suffering. We recognize suffering as it is, call it by its true name, and practice so that we can identify the deep causes of suffering. The division in families, the violence in schools and in society—all these things have to be confronted directly with our mindfulness. With mindfulness, we can look deeply into the nature of suffering and see how it has been made.

NURTURING MINDFULNESS

Mindfulness can be nurtured in many ways. If you tape an autumn leaf to your bathroom mirror, then every morning when you see it, the leaf will remind you to smile. While you wash your face and brush your teeth, you will be relaxed and mindful. A bell from a nearby church or even the telephone can help you to generate mindfulness. If you let the phone ring two or three times before answering, then you can breathe and return to your true self.

PRESENT MOMENT,
WONDERFUL MOMENT

We must make the present moment the most wonderful moment of our life because it's the only moment available to us. Looking deeply, we know that if we continue to live in the way we may have been living for the past twenty years—not mindfully, always running, always trying to escape—then the most wonderful moment of our life won't arrive. If we know how to go back to the present moment and be fully alive, then that moment is the most wonderful moment of our life. We have the capacity to do this. Through simple practices like walking, breathing, or smiling, we touch the beauty of life with mindfulness. We can make paradise available to us in the here and now.

THE HEART OF OUR PRACTICE

Once mindfulness is lit up, it can transform all the other mental formations. Every mental formation is sensitive to the energy of mindfulness. When it's a wholesome mental formation, mindfulness will help it grow and flourish. When a mental formation is negative, the energy of mindfulness can transform it into something positive. Mindfulness is the very heart of our practice.

BREATHE AS A FREE PERSON

You can practice freedom every moment of your daily life. Every step you take can help you reclaim your freedom. Every breath you take can help you develop and cultivate your freedom. When you eat, eat as a free person. When you walk, walk as a free person. When you breathe, breathe as a free person. This is possible anywhere.

WHEN MINDFULNESS
SHINES

Thanks to the sun, vegetables can grow. There are other conditions for the growth of plants, like rain and soil, but the sun is the primary source of energy for living things.

When mindfulness arises, it can transform other mental formations. Mindfulness is like the sun. It only has to shine its light to do its work.

POWERFUL THOUGHTS

As soon as you produce a thought, it will have an impact on your body, on your mind, and on the world. It will have an impact on your physical and mental health. A thought of compassion, understanding, nondiscrimination, or joy always helps our body and mind to heal. Thoughts and words of hatred, fear, or despair always have a harmful impact on our physical and mental health. Thoughts have the power to heal or to destroy. You can heal yourself just by thinking and speaking. Mindfulness helps us recognize the nature of our thoughts, speech, and actions.

OUR BREATH, A BRIDGE

Our breath is like a bridge connecting our bodies and our minds. In our daily lives, our bodies may be in one place and our minds somewhere else—in the past or in the future. This is called a state of distraction. Breathing connects the body and the mind. When you begin to breathe in and out mindfully, your body will come back to your mind, and your mind will go back to your body. You will be able to realize the oneness of body and mind and become fully present and fully alive in the here and now. You will be in a position to touch life deeply in the moment. This isn't difficult. Everyone can do it.

MINDFULNESS AS
MEDICINE

There are many kinds of medicine, but most of them only ease the suffering in our bodies and minds temporarily. They don't usually heal the source of our illness. Mindfulness, however, is a truly healing balm. It can help us heal ourselves, heal our planet, and put an end to our sense of alienation. If we can ground ourselves, become one with the earth, and treat her with care, she will nourish us and heal our bodies and minds. Our physical and mental sicknesses will be cured, and we'll have well-being in body and spirit.

HAPPINESS IS MADE OF
THESE MOMENTS

Happiness is made of these moments of mindfulness and concentration. When you're happy, when you have enough mindfulness and concentration, you feel good within yourself. You feel that you're in the Kingdom of God and then you can help other living beings.

HEALING OURSELVES,
HEALING THE EARTH

The practice of mindfulness helps us deeply enjoy every moment of life. If we practice mindful breathing, we can connect with the wonders of our body. When we can connect with our body, we can connect with the earth. And when we connect with the earth, we can connect with the whole cosmos. The practice of mindfulness helps us to touch Mother Earth inside of our bodies. The healing of our bodies and minds must go together with the healing of the earth.

THE ENERGY WITHIN US

Wherever there is mindfulness, there is life, understanding, and compassion. That is why the energy of mindfulness, the energy of the Buddha, is equivalent to the Holy Spirit. The Holy Spirit is the energy of love. We have that energy within us. When we say, "God is in my heart," we mean exactly that. Mindfulness is there if we know how to nurture and develop it. We know that we have the Holy Spirit within us to help us heal, transform, and bring happiness to people around us.

THIS IS IT

The opportunity that you have been waiting for is right here in the present moment. Each breath is that opportunity—an opportunity for you to go back to the now and stop your endless wandering.

The day that you've been waiting for is today; the moment that you've been waiting for is this very moment.

BEING AWARE OF WHAT
WE'RE DOING

To be mindful is to be truly present with your body and your mind, to bring harmony to your intentions and actions, and to be in harmony with those around you. We don't need to make a separate time for this outside of our daily activities. Mindfulness is the continuous practice of touching deeply every moment of daily life. We can practice mindfulness in the kitchen, the toilet, in our bedroom, and as we're going from one place to another. We can carry mindfulness with us as we wash the dishes, take a morning shower, or drive the car. We can do the same things we always do—walking, sitting, working, eating, and so on—with mindful awareness of what we're doing. Our mind is with our actions.

EACH BOWL I WASH IS A MIRACLE

To my mind, the idea that doing dishes is unpleasant can occur only when you aren't doing them. Once you're standing in front of the sink with your sleeves rolled up and your hands in warm water, it really isn't so bad. I enjoy taking my time with each dish, being fully aware of the dish, the water, and each movement of my hands. I know that if I hurry to go and have a cup of tea, the time will be unpleasant and not worth living. That would be a pity, for each minute, each second of life is a miracle. The dishes themselves and the fact that I'm here washing them are miracles! Each bowl I wash, each poem I compose, each time I invite a bell to sound is a miracle, and each has exactly the same value.

THICH NHAT HANH

MINDFULNESS IS THE ELEMENT OF HOLINESS IN US

Suppose you're boiling water to make coffee in the morning. You can use that time to practice. You become aware of each act, each movement, the whole time you're making coffee. You smile at every act, however small it is. It's a joy to live your daily life and know how to light the lamp of mindfulness, shining it on each moment, each act of the day. Mindfulness is the element of holiness within us. It isn't something abstract.

I HEAR ALREADY

Anything that can help you wake up has buddha nature. When I'm alone and a bird calls me, I return to myself. I breathe and smile, and sometimes it calls me once more. I smile and I say to the bird, "I hear already."

A LIBERATING SMILE

You may think that a smile is nothing, but it's a lot. With a true smile, you make all the generations of ancestors in you smile. It is liberation; it is transformation. Every mindful in-breath, every mindful out-breath, every peaceful step, every smile is an act of liberation.

PLENTY OF TIME

Caught up in the pressures of our daily lives, we can often feel as if we don't have any time to practice mindfulness. Breathing in and out mindfully, letting go of our thoughts, and becoming grounded in our own body, however, take only one or two minutes. We can practice all day long and benefit right away, whether sitting on the bus, driving a car, taking a shower, or cooking breakfast. We cannot say, "I have no time to practice." We have plenty of time if we know where to look.

MINDFUL DRINKING

There can be mindfulness in anything you do. While you're drinking a cup of water, if you know in that moment that you're drinking water and you aren't thinking of anything else, you're drinking mindfully. If you focus your whole being, body, and mind on the water, there is mindfulness and concentration, and the act of drinking may be described as mindful drinking. You drink not only with your mouth but with your body and your consciousness, too. Everyone is capable of drinking their water mindfully.

THE CAPACITY TO REST
AND DO NOTHING

We would all like to have the time to sit and appreciate the stillness that comes from doing nothing. But if we were given the time, would we be able to be still and quiet? That is the problem with many of us. We complain that we don't have the time to rest, to enjoy being there. But we're used to always doing something. We have no capacity to rest and do nothing. We are workaholics. That is why learning how to be right where we are without doing anything is a very important practice. It's also a very challenging one.

HEALING FROM OVERWORK

When we get home from work, we may notice that our body is full of stress and tension. Our body is suffering because we have not taken good care of it. We have worked it too hard. We have brought many toxins into our body by the way we eat, drink, work, and overwork. Mindful breathing brings the elements of peace and harmony into our breath. Whether we're lying down, sitting, or standing, the elements of stress, conflict, and tension can be released slowly through mindful breathing.

THEN GO WASH
THE DISHES

If someone were to have asked my teacher what the main idea of Buddhism is, he might have answered, "Did you have breakfast?" When the student said yes, my teacher might have said, "Then go wash the dishes." Having breakfast is a living reality; we have to live deeply our breakfast eating. And if we've finished our breakfast, we live deeply our dishwashing instead of trying to find the meaning in things that are so far away.

THICH NHAT HANH

THERE IS ONLY
TOOTHBRUSHING

When you brush your teeth in the morning, brush them in such a way that happiness is possible during the whole time of brushing, which may last only one or two minutes. That is something I do every morning and after each meal. I brush my teeth in such a way that happiness is real during the time of brushing. I don't say, "Let us brush quickly so we can go do this or that." Brushing your teeth is a practice. You can be in paradise during the time of toothbrushing.

DO YOU FEEL AT REST
IN YOUR RESTROOM?

Whatever else you do during the day, you probably use the restroom. It's interesting that in the United States you call it the restroom; do you feel restful in your restroom? In France, they used to call it *la cabine d'aisance*. "Aisance" means ease; you feel at ease, you feel comfortable. So when you go to the restroom, feel at ease with it; enjoy your time in the restroom. That's my practice.

THE TEACHING IS
LOVELY, ALWAYS

The basic thing is to receive and bring the practice into our daily life. The Buddha said, "The teaching is lovely in the beginning, in the middle, and in the end." If it's the right practice, then it can bring relief and joy right away.

LIFE IS PRESENT

A function of mindfulness is recognizing that life is already here. You can have real contact with life and make it meaningful and deep. When you are present, life is also present. Suppose you're watching a beautiful sunset with a group of people. Many of them are concentrating on the wonders of the sunset and contemplating them. But maybe one or two people, obsessed by their worries and fears, aren't really present. For them, the beautiful sunset isn't available as it is to the other people in the group. When you are truly present, life is also present. We have an appointment with life in the present moment. We have to be present in this moment so we don't miss our appointment.

PEACE IS HERE

Peace can exist only in the present moment. It's ridiculous to say, "Wait until I finish this, then I will be free to live in peace." What is "this"? A diploma, a job, a house, the payment of a debt? If you think that way, peace will never come. There is always another "this" that will follow the present one. If you aren't living in peace at this moment, you will never be able to. If you truly want to be at peace, you must be at peace right now. Otherwise, there is only the hope of peace someday.

OUR IDEA OF HAPPINESS

Each of us is caught in an idea of happiness. We believe that we'll be truly happy when certain conditions are fulfilled. We don't realize that this idea is an obstacle to our true happiness. If we can release our idea of happiness, true happiness is born in us right away. We set up conditions for our happiness and become trapped. Happiness can come to us at any time if we're free. Why do we commit ourselves to only one idea of happiness? If we let go of that idea, happiness will come to us from every direction.

THE SECRET

The now is the only moment when and where you can find what you have been looking for. You have been searching for *nirvana*. You have been looking for God. You have been looking for enlightenment, for awakening. You have been looking for the Pure Land and for your true nature of no birth and no death. It turns out that everything you have been looking for already exists in the present moment. The secret is to go back to the now.

THIS MOMENT IS
NO DREAM

The present moment is more beautiful than any kind of dream. This moment is no dream. This is reality. Pinch yourself—doesn't it hurt? You aren't dreaming. You're fully awake. You have had so many dreams, but no dream is as beautiful as the reality that is unfolding itself to you in the here and now.

A MATTER OF PRACTICE

Peace is all around us in the world and in nature, and it's within us in our body and our spirit. Once we learn to touch this peace, we'll be healed and transformed. It isn't a matter of faith; it's a matter of practice. We need only to find ways to bring our body and mind back to the present moment so we can touch what is refreshing, healing, and wondrous.

WE BECOME OURSELVES

We don't have to die to enter the kingdom of heaven. In fact we have to be fully alive. When we breathe in and out and hug a beautiful tree, we're in heaven. When we take one conscious breath, aware of our eyes, our heart, our liver, and our non-toothache, we're transported to paradise right away. Peace is available. We only have to touch it. When we touch peace, everything becomes real. We become ourselves, fully alive in the present moment, and the tree, our child, and everything else reveal themselves to us in their full splendor.

LIVING HAPPILY IN THE PRESENT MOMENT

The practice of resting, of stopping, is crucial. If we cannot rest, it's because we have not stopped. We have continued to run. We think that happiness and well-being aren't possible in the here and the now. We have received the seed of that belief from our parents and our grandparents. They struggled all their lives and believed that happiness was only possible in the future. But the teaching of the Buddha is that you can be happy right here, right now. The conditions for your well-being and happiness can be found in the here and now. This is the teaching of living happily in the present moment.

THE WILLINGNESS TO STOP
ISN'T THE SAME AS STOPPING

You cannot stop just because you want to stop. The willingness to stop isn't the same as stopping. You need to have some insight to really stop. It's like relaxation—every one of us knows that relaxation is good for us. The tension in your body has been accumulating for a long time, and you want to relieve it. You have the desire to release the tension, and you try to do it, but you cannot because the willingness to relax isn't relaxation. You need to have some insight to relax and release the tension.

GO WITHOUT RUSHING

Perhaps you don't feel well in body and mind because you have not touched that peace, that beauty, that wonder of life that is available in you and around you. You feel that energy pushing you to go somewhere, to do something so that you can be happy and free. But freedom is obtained when you stop running. You have something to do; it's okay to do it. You have somewhere to go; you may like to go there. But why do you have to rush?

GIVE YOURSELF TIME
TO BE FREE

Suppose you need to be at the airport at ten o'clock.
You think that you have time to linger and wait until
later to leave your house. But maybe there is heavy
traffic, you arrive late, and you have to run. You can
always plan so that you have plenty of time to walk as
a free person at the airport. It should become a habit
to plan so that we have plenty of time to do each thing.
That's a good habit that everyone can have.

HAPPINESS DEPENDS ON OUR AWARENESS

Most of the time, our vision gives rise to a neutral feeling. Yet someone who has lost their sight would give anything to be able to see, and if suddenly they could, they would consider it a miraculous gift. We who have eyes capable of seeing many forms and colors are often unhappy. If we want to practice, we can go out and look at leaves, flowers, children, and clouds, and we can be happy. Whether or not we're happy depends on our awareness.

ENJOYING A CARROT

Some of us, while looking at a carrot, can see the sunshine, the earth, and the whole cosmos in it. It has come from the whole cosmos for our nourishment. You may like to smile at it before you put it in your mouth. When you chew it, be aware that you're chewing a piece of carrot. Don't put anything else into your mouth, like your projects, your worries, your fear; just put the carrot in. And when you chew, chew only the carrot, not your projects or your ideas. You're capable of living in the present moment, in the here and now. It's simple, but you need some training to just enjoy the carrot. That is a miracle.

BREATHING WITH AWARENESS

When a person breathes in and breathes out with awareness, this is called mindfulness of breathing. This isn't our usual way of breathing. Every day, all of us breathe in and out without stopping. But that isn't the Dharma. When we breathe in and know that we're breathing in, when we breathe out and know that we're breathing out, that is the true living Dharma.

THE LIVING DHARMA

The living Dharma is different from the spoken Dharma and the written Dharma. The written Dharma and the spoken Dharma are there only to help us generate the living Dharma. We should live our daily life in such a way that the living Dharma inhabits us in every moment. Brushing our teeth, taking a shower, cooking our breakfast—we do these things so that the living Dharma is with us all the time.

DON'T KILL TIME

Every second of life is filled with precious jewels. Those jewels are our awareness of the sky, the earth, the trees, the hills, the rivers, the oceans, and all the miracles around us. We don't want to kill time. We want to profit as much as we can from the time that is given us to live. Each morning when we wake up to life, we see that we have a gift of a brand-new twenty-four hours. If we have mindfulness, concentration, and insight, we can live those twenty-four hours fully and joyfully. In twenty-four hours, we can generate the energy of understanding and compassion that will benefit ourselves, our planet, and each person we come into contact with.

TIME IS LIFE

We want to treasure every moment of our life; we want to treasure every minute. We don't need to forget time. We don't want time to move quickly because time is life.

THE DISEASE
OF OUR TIMES

If you're restless, if you can't sit peacefully and with
stability, it's because you aren't established in the now.
Restlessness is the disease of our times, and the more
we try to fill it with the consumption of things—such
as food and drink, movies, websites, books, or games—
the more emptiness grows, and the more restless we
become. We should remind each other that the now is
the only thing that is solid and real.

REALITY, NOT
SUPERSTITION

As practitioners, our aim isn't to make a lot of money. Our aim is to transform the suffering in our heart; to live in equanimity, peace, and happiness; and to offer happiness to our family and those around us. Our happiness multiplies exponentially when we see that we can bring happiness to those around us. This is reality, not superstition.

BECOME LIKE A CHILD

Children have the capacity to be in the here and now more than adults. They don't think too much about the future. They don't create a lot of projects like we do, and they aren't caught up in the past. So learning to be more like children is a good practice.

STEP IN THE DIRECTION
OF LIFE

There is no need for us to struggle to arrive somewhere else. We know that our final destination is the cemetery. Why are we in a hurry to get there? Why not step in the direction of life, which is in the present moment?

DO NOTHING;
LIBERATION WILL FOLLOW

A buddha is a person who has no more business to do and isn't looking for anything. In doing nothing, in simply stopping, we can live freely and be true to ourselves, and our liberation will contribute to the liberation of all beings.

BODY AND MIND
GO TOGETHER

If we don't return to, take hold of, and master the mind, we cause suffering to ourselves and those around us. Mastering our mind brings great benefit and happiness. To master the mind, we first have to grasp the body. The body and the mind go together. The breath belongs to the body, just as the two feet and legs belong to the body. If we can grasp and be in touch with our breath and our footsteps, then we'll slowly get hold of the mind.

A STATE OF ONENESS

When you spend two hours with your computer, you may forget entirely that you have a body. And when your mind isn't with your body, you cannot be truly alive; you're lost in your work, in your worry, your fear, and your projects. By breathing in mindfully and bringing the mind home to the body, we become fully alive. When we bring our mind home to our body, our mind becomes one with our body. Our body becomes a mindful body, and our mind becomes an embodied mind. This state of oneness of body and mind allows us to get back in touch with the wonders of life, and our body is the first wonder of life that we encounter.

THERE IS AWAKENING

When we breathe in and bring our mind back to our body, when we're truly present—body and mind united—there is awakening. We know we're alive; we're present, and life is there for us to live. That is already a kind of awakening. So awakening isn't something very far away, but we need to bring our mind back to our body and be truly there in the present moment.

THE MOST PRECIOUS
PRACTICE

Meditation is being aware of what's going on: in your body, in your feelings, in your mind, and in the world. The most precious practice in Buddhism is meditation, and it's important to practice meditation in a joyful mood. We have to smile a lot to meditate.

ENJOY SITTING HERE

If you allow your body to sit in a relaxing, peaceful way, it calms your body and mind. Effortlessness is the key to success. Sitting like this allows you to enjoy your in-breath and out-breath, to enjoy being alive, to enjoy sitting here.

MEDITATION BRINGS
HAPPINESS

Meditation brings happiness. This happiness comes,
first, from the fact that you're master of yourself, no
longer caught up in forgetfulness. If you follow your
breathing and allow a half-smile to blossom, mindful
of your feelings and thoughts, the movements of your
body will naturally become gentler and more relaxed.
Harmony will be there, and true happiness will arise.

LIVING FULLY AND DEEPLY

Keeping our mind present in each moment is the foundation of meditation practice. When we achieve this, we live our lives fully and deeply, seeing things that others in forgetfulness do not.

STOP AND BREATHE

Just as the lampshade stops the light from dispersing
so you can read your book more easily, the first step of
meditation is stopping—stopping the dispersion and
concentrating on one subject. The best subject, the
most available subject, is your breathing. Breathing is
wonderful. Whether you count breaths or just follow
them, breathing unites body and mind.

DWELLING IN PEACE
AND FREEDOM

All you need to do is focus your attention on your in-breath and out-breath, recognize it, and smile to it. Being aware that you're breathing in means you're really there. Your presence is a wonder and a miracle. Breathing like that, you bring your mind back to your body and become truly present in the now. Treasuring that moment, you dwell in peace and freedom. Each breath is a miracle. Each breath has the power to nourish and to heal.

A HIGHLY RECOMMENDED PRACTICE

The Buddha said that before he became fully enlightened, he enjoyed the practice of mindful breathing. It helped him to be relaxed and free and not get tired. That's why after he became fully enlightened, he continued to practice mindful breathing. He recommended this practice to all his students.

BREATHING IN, I KNOW
THAT I AM BREATHING IN

Breathing in, I know that I am breathing in.
Breathing out, I know that I am breathing out.
In...Out...

Enjoy your in-breath and your out-breath. If you do this very simple exercise correctly, it yields miracles. Be at one with your in-breath and your out-breath. Be fully alive—fully present in the here and the now. This is a miracle that you can perform at any time. When you breathe with mindfulness and concentration, life becomes present. You stop thinking about everything else and become one with your breathing. It's wonderful. After a few minutes doing this practice, the quality of your breathing automatically improves.

WHY NOT SMILE?

While following your breathing, you've been able to
stay fully conscious for some time. You have succeeded
a bit, haven't you? So why not smile? A tiny bud
of a smile, just to prove you have succeeded. Seeing
you smile, I know immediately that you're dwelling
in awareness. Keep this smile always blooming, the
half-smile of a buddha.

NO MORE THINKING

Mindfulness of breathing is very practical, and everyone can do it. It isn't complicated, and it brings a lot of calm and happiness right away. When you use your mind to identify the in-breath and out-breath, there is no more thinking. "Breathing in, I know this is an in-breath"—that isn't thinking. That is recognizing what is going on: your in-breath and your out-breath. Please enjoy your in-breath and your out-breath.

TO SIT ISN'T ENOUGH

To sit is not enough. We have to be at the same time. To be what? To be is to be something; you cannot be nothing. To eat, you have to eat something. You cannot eat nothing. To be aware is to be aware of something. To be angry is to be angry at something. So to be is to be something, and that something is what is going on in your body, in your mind, in your feelings, and in the world.

THE BELL OF MINDFULNESS

The bell of mindfulness is the voice of the Buddha calling us back to ourselves. We have to respect that sound, stop our thinking and talking, and go back to ourselves with a smile and our mindful breathing. It isn't a buddha from the outside. It's our own buddha who calls us. If we cannot hear the sound of the bell, then we cannot hear other sounds, which also come from the Buddha: the sound of the wind, the sound of the bird, even the sounds of cars or a baby crying. They are all a call from the Buddha to return to ourselves.

PRACTICE GOING HOME
ALL DAY LONG

In Plum Village, every time you hear the bell, you stop thinking, you stop talking, you stop doing things. You pay attention to your in-breath as you breathe in and you say, "I listen, I listen. This wonderful sound brings me back to my true home." My true home is inside. My true home is in the here and now. So practicing going home is what we do all day long because we're only comfortable in our true home. Our true home is available, and we can go home at any moment. Our home should be safe, intimate, and cozy, and it's we who make it that way.

TAKING REFUGE IN
SOMETHING REAL

The Buddha taught that inside us there's an island where we can take refuge. When we feel lost, lonely, sad, hesitant, or desperate we can come back to that island and have safety. That island is our stable mind. That island isn't a place outside us. One breath can bring us back to that island immediately. In each person there are seeds of stability, freedom, and nonfear. It's these seeds that make a place of refuge for us and protect us. When we take refuge in our island, we're taking refuge in something real.

YOU ARE SAFE

You enter your inner island through your in-breath and out-breath. You learn to extricate yourself from all fears, worries, and anxieties. The more you dwell in that island within, through the in-breath and out-breath, and let go of fears, notions, and dispersion, the more that island will grow. Even when life goes up and down with coming, going, gaining, and losing, you dwell in your inner island, and you are safe.

SIT LIKE A MOUNTAIN

Meditation isn't for avoiding problems or running away from difficulties. We don't practice escaping. We practice so that we have enough strength to confront problems effectively. To do this, we must be calm, fresh, and solid. That is why we need to practice the art of stopping. When we learn to stop, we become calmer, and our mind becomes clearer, like clear water after the particles of mud have settled. Sitting quietly, just breathing in and out, we develop strength, concentration, and clarity. So sit like a mountain. No wind can blow the mountain down. If you can sit for half an hour, enjoy sitting for half an hour. If you can sit for a few minutes, enjoy sitting for a few minutes. That is already good.

TRUE DILIGENCE

Many people think that you have to practice sitting meditation all day, until you feel pain in your whole body, to be a diligent practitioner.

This isn't the practice of true diligence. You don't have to suffer to progress in the practice. In our practice, true diligence, wholesome energy, and effort are born from joy. The point of the practice isn't to create more suffering, but to bring well-being, transformation, and healing. We aren't practicing only to achieve some better state in the future, but to get in touch with the joy and peace that are available right now, in every moment. If you practice with the correct attitude, you will feel relief from suffering right away.

NON-PRACTICE

We tend to think that we have to do something to heal ourselves. But sitting with mindfulness and concentration is doing something. Just allow yourself to sit quietly and be yourself. Don't strive; relaxation will come. When you're completely relaxed, healing will take place on its own. There is no healing without relaxation. And relaxation means doing nothing. Just allow your breathing to follow its natural rhythm. Healing begins when you aren't trying to do anything. This is the practice of non-practice.

BREATH ENJOYING ITSELF

We cannot describe the practice as breath work.
We aren't working on our breath. We allow our breath
to enjoy itself. This is mindfulness of breathing. It's
like the vegetation and the sunshine. The sunshine
just embraces the vegetation. It has an impact on the
vegetation, but the work of the sunshine is to shine
on the vegetation and embrace it. We do the same
thing with our breathing. We don't try to change our
breathing. We just become aware of our in-breath and
out-breath as our in-breath and out-breath.

CELEBRATING LIFE

Sitting meditation is a way to celebrate life. We celebrate with our in-breath and our out-breath, and we can smile. We don't try to become a buddha. We just enjoy sitting and accept ourselves as we are.

DON'T WORK TOO HARD

Buddhism should not be hard work. If we do sitting meditation and exert too much effort, that isn't correct practice. If while we're eating, we try not to speak and try to pick up food in a very proper way, then we're working too hard. We should be mindful and live our lives with as much relaxation as possible.

THAT'S ALL IT TAKES

We all know how to sit and how to breathe. That's all we have to do. After only a few moments of concentrating on our breathing, we can bring peace and calm to our body and mind. We only need to pay attention to our in-breath and out-breath. Focus on that. That's all it takes to begin to calm the agitation in your mind and body. You only need to dwell peacefully in your in-breath and out-breath for a short while, and you will begin to restore stability and peace within yourself.

REMEMBER THAT YOU
HAVE A BODY

Awareness of your breathing brings your mind back to your body. Be with your body and remember that you have a body. Release any tension and bring calm to your body. This is the first step in restoring wellness. Bringing your mind home to your body, you become established in the here and now, and you have a chance to experience each moment deeply. When you're in touch with your body, you're in touch with life, the cosmos, and planet Earth.

I KNOW YOU ARE THERE

How much time do we spend going back to our body, holding it tenderly with the energy of mindfulness, and smiling to it? Each of us knows that we need to do this a lot. We need to spend time holding our body with our awareness very tenderly, with a lot of compassion, and smiling to it with a smile of recognition. "Oh my body, I know you are there. I will take good care of you." Let us practice holding our body with mindfulness and smiling.

THIS WE CALL INSIGHT

When we meditate on our body, we live with it as truth and give it our most lucid attention; we become one with it. The flower blossoms because sunlight touches and warms its bud, becoming one with it. Meditation reveals not a concept of truth but a direct view of truth itself. This we call insight, the kind of understanding based on attention and concentration.

ENLIGHTENMENT ALREADY

Suppose you are breathing in, concentrated on your in-breath, and you know "Ah, I'm breathing in"— that is enlightenment already. "I am alive because I'm breathing in, because those who have died don't breathe in anymore. And since I'm breathing in, I am alive." "I'm still alive" is an insight.

DON'T FORGET
YOUR HEART

When you use the energy of mindfulness to embrace your heart and smile to it, you see that your heart is still functioning normally. That is a wonderful thing. Many people wish they had a heart that functioned normally. It's the basic condition for our well-being, another condition for our happiness. When we hold our heart with the energy of mindfulness, our heart is comforted. We have neglected our heart for a long time. We think only of other things. We run after things that we believe to be the true conditions for happiness and we forget our heart.

> BREATHING IN, I AM AWARE OF MY HEART.
> BREATHING OUT, I SMILE TO MY HEART.

RECEIVE THE ENERGY

Our true home is right here, but sometimes we can't find it because it's hidden by the tension and pain in our bodies and minds. If we know how to relax, we can release the tension, open our mind and body, and let the energy of mindfulness bring relief to our pain and suffering. We don't have to do much. We just bring our mind back to our body, become fully present in the here and now, and allow our body to receive the energy. If we have pain, sorrow, fear, and anger in our mind and in our heart, it is possible to let the collective energy of a wholesome, mindful community bring relief to those emotions.

A BATH OF MINDFULNESS

If we have enough mindfulness to recognize, embrace, and look deeply into our anger, we may allow it to come up during sitting meditation. "Breathing in, I know anger has manifested in me. Breathing out, I embrace my anger with all my tenderness." "Breathing in, I'm aware that anger is still in me. Breathing out, I'm taking good care of my anger." It's like a big sister holding her younger sister, like a mother holding a baby. Even if we haven't practiced deeply enough to see the nature of our anger and transform it, our anger will lose some of its strength after bathing it in mindfulness. That's exactly what we do—we give our anger, our fear, our despair a bath of mindfulness.

THE CHANCE TO DO
NOTHING

We can learn a lot from observing what is going on in our body and mind during sitting meditation. But sitting also gives us a chance to do nothing. We just enjoy sitting and breathing in and out. "Breathing in, I know I'm alive. Breathing out, I smile to life in me and around me."

INFORMAL MEDITATION

You don't have to do mindful breathing in the sitting position. Suppose you are standing in line waiting to copy something at work or waiting to talk with a colleague. You may be out at lunch or waiting in line to get coffee or tea. You can still practice mindful breathing and focus on enjoying yourself and the people around you. Meditation can be very informal.

DECOMPARTMENTALIZING
OUR LIVES

If a doctor gives you an injection, not only your arm but your whole body benefits from it. If you practice sitting one hour a day, that hour should benefit all twenty-four hours. One smile, one breath should be for the benefit of the whole day, not just that moment. We must practice in a way that removes the barrier between practice and non-practice.

OUR HAPPINESS IS
BOUNDLESS

As we sit, we may become aware that there are many stars outside in the sky. We may not be able to see them, but they are there. We're sitting on an amazingly beautiful planet, which is revolving in our galaxy, the Milky Way, a river containing trillions of stars. If we're able to have this awareness when we sit, then what else do we need to sit for? We see all the wonders of the universe and our planet Earth very clearly. When we sit with this kind of awareness, we can embrace the whole world, from the past to the future. And when we sit like that, our happiness is boundless.

REVERENCE FOR OUR BODY

When we practice looking deeply into our body, we
discover its nature of interbeing. It's made of all the
elements: earth, water, fire, air, space, and time. And
we begin to see the mountains, the rivers, the trees, the
flowers, the dew, the stars, the galaxies—everything
in our body. The whole cosmos is there in it. And
suddenly we see our body as something to bow down
to. We discover deep reverence, and we learn to handle
our body with respect.

THE ALTAR OF THE SPIRIT

Before we realize the interbeing nature of our body, we don't really know what it is. We may think it's the cause of all our problems and despise it. Those who hate their body don't know its value. They don't know that the body is also the mind and the altar of the spirit. We may have a complex that our body is less beautiful than other people's bodies. It's only with the practice of looking deeply that we can remove all types of complexes. Looking deeply, we develop profound respect because our body is nothing less than a miracle, a wonder, a manifestation of the cosmos.

OUR PRACTICE IS SIMPLE

Our practice is simple: mindfulness in our daily life. We practice the meditation techniques of stopping and looking deeply. We do this to keep from being pulled along in many directions. Too often we're carried along by the energy of the people around us, by circumstances, by our own thoughts, and we don't have the strength to go against these forces. Ask yourself, "What have I done with my life over the past few years?" If you have not practiced stopping, the years will seem to have gone by like a dream. You may never have stopped for a moment to look at the moon or hold a flower in your hands. Without stopping and looking deeply, we can't really live our lives.

SELF-HEALING

The practices of quiet, peaceful sitting, peaceful walking, and mindful breathing help bring peace and relaxation to our body. They will enhance our power to heal. They restore our immune system. We have elements of healing available in us. When we can produce a thought of compassion, understanding, or forgiveness, that's an element of healing. Every in-breath and out-breath that releases tension in the body and brings joy into our daily life is an element of healing.

IT IS NOT A MEANS—
IT IS AN END

When we practice mindfulness, every practice should be an end in itself. Suppose you are practicing mindful breathing. You think that breathing mindfully will bring healing. But you have to breathe in such a way that every breath is itself an act of healing. It is not a means—it is an end. If we breathe an in-breath and feel calm and pleasant, then we are healing.

JUST REST

We know that when an animal is wounded, it looks for a quiet place to lie down. Wisdom is present in the animal's body. It knows that rest is the best way to heal. It doesn't do anything, not even eat or hunt; it just lies down. Some days later, it can get up. It's healed. Human beings have lost confidence in their body. We panic and try to do many different things. We worry too much about our body. We don't allow it to heal itself. We don't know how to rest. Mindful breathing helps us to relearn the art of resting. Mindful breathing is like a loving mother holding her sick baby in her arms saying, "Don't worry, I'll take good care of you; just rest."

BREATHING AND STOPPING

For healing to take place, your in-breath has to be able to stop you from running. You learn to breathe in such a way that your in-breath becomes pleasant and you want to keep your attention on it. You learn to find peace, happiness, and joy in your in-breath. If you can do that, then you can stop running. But if you breathe in with the desire to get something from your in-breath—such as health—you're still running.

A RIVER OF PERCEPTIONS

Our thoughts, feelings, and perceptions flow like a river. If we try to stop the flow of the river, we'll meet the resistance of the water. It's better to flow with it, and then we may be able to guide it in ways we want it to go. We must not attempt to halt it. We must be aware of every little stream that joins it. We must be aware of all the thoughts, feelings, and sensations that arise in us—of their birth, duration, and disappearance. Do you see? The river of perceptions is still flowing but no longer in darkness. It is now flowing in the sunlight of awareness. To keep this sun always shining inside of us—illuminating each rivulet, each pebble, each bend in the river—is the practice of meditation.

LAY DOWN YOUR SWORD

When we meditate, we seem to have two selves. One is the flowing river of thoughts and feelings, and the other is the sun of awareness that shines on them. Which is our own self? Which is true? Which false? Which is good? Which bad? Please calm down, my friend. Lay down your sharp sword of conceptual thinking. Don't be in such a hurry to cut your self in two. Both are self. Neither is true. Neither is false. They are both true and both false.

PRACTICE ILLUSTRATIONS

The practice of meditation isn't an exercise in analysis or reasoning. The sword of logic has no place in the practice of awareness, concentration, and understanding. In Vietnam, when we cook a pot of dried corn, we concentrate the fire under the pot. Several hours later the kernels come loose and split open. When the sun's rays beat down on the snow, the snow slowly melts. When a hen sits on her eggs, the chicks inside gradually take form until they are ready to peck their way out. These images illustrate the effect of practicing meditation.

DON'T TURN YOUR MIND
INTO A BATTLEFIELD

Throughout your meditation, keep the sun of your awareness shining. Our awareness lights our every thought and feeling and allows us to recognize them, to be aware of their birth, duration, and dissolution without judging or evaluating, welcoming or banishing them. It's important that you don't consider awareness to be your "ally," called on to suppress the "enemies" that are your unruly thoughts. Don't turn your mind into a battlefield; don't have a war there. All your feelings—joy, sorrow, anger, hatred—are part of yourself.

FEAR, MY OLD FRIEND

If fear wishes to come up, don't ignore it. Greet it
warmly with your mindfulness. "Fear, my old friend,
I recognize you." If you're afraid of your fear, it may
overwhelm you. But if you invite it up calmly and smile
at it mindfully, it will lose some of its strength. After
you have practiced watering the seeds of mindfulness
for a few weeks, you will be strong enough to invite
your fear to come up any time, and you will be able
to embrace it with your mindfulness. It may not be
entirely pleasant, but with mindfulness you're safe.

MERE RECOGNITION

When we're rooted in mindfulness, we can see clearly what is unfolding within us. We don't grasp at it, and we don't push it away—we simply recognize it. When we're angry, mindfulness recognizes the anger. When we're jealous, mindfulness recognizes the jealousy. When we acknowledge the presence of fear or sadness in us, we don't judge it and say that it's bad. We simply observe every occurrence in our body and mind with our mindfulness and greet whatever arises without praise, reprimand, or judgment. This is called mere recognition. Mere recognition doesn't take sides. The object of recognition isn't our enemy. It's none other than ourselves. We acknowledge it as we would acknowledge our own child.

THICH NHAT HANH

EMBRACING PAIN

If you embrace a minor pain with mindfulness, it will
be transformed in a few minutes. Just breathe in and
out and smile at it. But when you have a block of pain
that is stronger, more time is needed. Practice sitting
and walking meditation while you embrace your pain in
mindfulness, and sooner or later it will be transformed.

TRANSFORMATION
AND HEALING

When mindfulness embraces pain, it begins to
penetrate and transform the pain, like sunshine
penetrating a flower bud and helping it to blossom.
When mindfulness touches something beautiful, it
reveals its beauty. When it touches something painful,
mindfulness transforms and heals it.

HANDLING THE SNAKE

Dealing with suffering is like handling a poisonous
snake. We have to learn about the snake, and we have
to grow stronger and more stable to handle it safely.
Then we'll be ready to confront the snake. If we never
confront it, one day it will surprise us, and we shall
die of a snakebite. The pain we carry in the depths of
our consciousness is similar. When the pain grows
big and confronts us, there is nothing we can do if
we haven't practiced to become strong and stable
in mindfulness. We should only invite our suffering
up when we're ready. Then, when it comes, we can
handle it. To transform our suffering, we don't struggle with it or try to get rid of it. We simply bathe it in
the light of our mindfulness.

MINDFULNESS, CONCENTRATION, AND INSIGHT

The energy of mindfulness carries within itself the energy of concentration. When you're mindful of something, whether that something is a flower, a friend, or a cup of tea, you become concentrated on the object of your mindfulness. The more you're mindful, the more concentrated you become. The energy of concentration is born from the energy of mindfulness. And if you're concentrated enough, the energy of concentration contains the energy of insight. Mindfulness, concentration, and insight are the energies that make up the Buddha. These three kinds of energy can transform our habit energies and lead to healing and nourishment.

RECOGNIZE IT AS YOURS
AND SMILE

Every one of us has habit energies that push us to say
and do things we don't want to say or do. Mindful
breathing can help you recognize habit energy when it
emerges. You don't have to fight that energy; you only
have to recognize it as yours and smile at it. That is
enough. "Hello there, my habit energy. I know you are
there, but you cannot do anything to me." You smile at
it, and then you're free. This is a wonderful protection.

WHY WAIT TO BE HAPPY?

Many people in our society aren't happy, even though the conditions for their happiness already exist. Their habit energy is always pushing them ahead, preventing them from being happy in the here and now. But with a little bit of training, we can all learn to recognize this energy every time it comes up. Why wait to be happy?

FILTERING THE WATER

If we're dying of thirst and someone brings us a glass of
muddy water, we know we must find a way to filter it
to survive. We can't just throw it away; that water, even
though it isn't pure, is our only hope of salvation. In
the same way, we have to accept all of our afflictions, all
of our mental formations, and all of our difficulties to
transform them. If we reject them, if we try to run away
from them, we'll never succeed. There is no escaping
the things we hate. We can only transform them into
what we love.

LOOKING AT A LOTUS FLOWER, SEEING THE MUD

It's only by looking deeply into the nature of our suffering that we'll be able to see the way out. If we try to run away from our suffering, we have no chance. We can learn a lot from our suffering. There is a beautiful flower called a lotus that grows from the mud at the bottom of a pond and blooms on the surface. When we look into a lotus flower, we see the mud. Happiness is a kind of lotus. Without the element of suffering, you cannot make happiness. This is one of the deepest teachings of mindfulness: this is because that is. Because there is mud, there can be a lotus.

THE MUSIC OF MINDFUL
BREATHING

There are moments when many mental formations want to manifest at the same time. Your jealousy wants to speak; your fear wants to speak; your anger wants to speak; and your mindfulness also wants to speak. It's like a group of people all wanting to talk at the same time. You aren't peaceful.

You're advised at that moment to play music. You say, "You will each have a chance to express yourself, but now let's listen to some music." And you play the music of mindful breathing: "Breathing in, breathing out, I have arrived, I am home, in the here and now." You have the instrument. If you play the music, everyone will calm down after just a few minutes.

PUTTING OUT THE FIRE

When you're angry, you usually pay careful attention to what the other person is saying and doing, but you don't pay enough attention to your own suffering. The more you listen to the other person, the angrier you become. That is why it's better not to do anything. Go back and take good care of your anger. When your house is on fire, the first thing you do is try to put the fire out—not run after the person you think started the fire.

TAKING CARE OF ANGER

To take care of my anger, I bring my attention to my breathing and look deeply inside myself. Right away, I notice an energy there called anger. Then I recognize that I need another kind of energy to take care of this anger; I invite that energy to come up to do that job. This second energy is called mindfulness. Every one of us has the seed of mindfulness within us. If we know how to touch that seed, we can begin to generate the energy of mindfulness, and with that energy, we can take good care of the energy of anger.

STEADY AND STRONG

When our mindfulness is strong and stable, we
don't have to wait for the seeds of suffering to arise
unexpectedly. We know they are lying there in the
basement of our consciousness. When the upper level
of our consciousness is unoccupied, ready to shine
the light of mindfulness on these seeds, we invite
them up. We invite up the sadness, despair, regret,
and longing that in the past have been difficult for
us to touch. We sit down and talk with them like old
friends. But before we invite them up, we must be
sure that the lamp of our mindfulness is lit and that
its light is steady and strong.

COMING HOME
TO OURSELVES

We're afraid of going home to ourselves because
we lack the tools or the means of self-protection.
Equipped with mindfulness, we can go home safely
and not be overwhelmed by our pain, sorrow, and
depression. Going home mindfully, we can talk to our
wounded child within using the following mantra:
"Darling, I have come home to you. I'm here for you. I
embrace you in my arms. I'm sorry that I left you alone
for a long time." With some training, with mindful
walking and mindful breathing, we'll be able to go
home and embrace our pain and sorrow.

BATHING IN THE LIGHT OF MINDFULNESS

If a bird has been hit by an arrow, it will be afraid
whenever it sees a bow. It won't even perch on a branch
that resembles the shape of a bow. If we were wounded
as a young child, the seeds of suffering we received
then are still with us today. The way we relate to life
in the present moment is partly based on these seeds
of suffering. Seeds from the past manifest in our mind
every day, but because we have not bathed them in the
light of mindfulness, we aren't aware of them. This
recognition alone will cause them to lose some of their
power over us.

UNDERSTANDING, COMPASSION, AND HEALING

Unless you listen to your suffering, unless you look deeply into your suffering and embrace it tenderly with your energy of mindfulness, you cannot understand the roots of your suffering. When you begin to understand the roots of your suffering, suddenly the energy of compassion, of understanding, arises. And understanding and compassion have the power to heal. By embracing and listening to your suffering, you bring about understanding and compassion. And when the nectar of compassion is born in you, you suffer less; you feel less lonely. You begin to feel the warmth within yourself. You're building a home inside yourself.

THANKS TO SUFFERING, UNDERSTANDING IS POSSIBLE

The fact is that, thanks to suffering, thanks to understanding the nature of suffering, we have a chance to cultivate our understanding and our compassion. Without suffering, we cannot learn to be understanding and compassionate. That is why suffering is noble. We should not allow suffering to overwhelm us. If we know how to look deeply into the nature of suffering and learn from it, then we have the wisdom of understanding and compassion.

THICH NHAT HANH

NOURISHED BY OUR COMPASSION

To nourish compassion is a wonderful practice. We become more relaxed and are immune to many kinds of disease. When you're angry and tense, you may get sick. But if you're full of compassion, you can smile; you can forgive. You won't become a victim of sickness. Compassion protects us not only from anger, fear, and unhappiness, but it also protects our body from sickness. That is why we should feed our compassion every day.

NOTHING CAN LIVE
WITHOUT FOOD

Looking deeply into our suffering, we can see the many causes and conditions that have brought it about. We also see what feeds that suffering, what we continue to bring into our body and mind that keep our suffering alive. Nothing can live without food. When we've seen what feeds our suffering, we can decide to stop ingesting it.

WITHOUT THE GARBAGE
THERE CAN BE NO ROSE

Happiness and unhappiness inter-are. Happiness can be present only if unhappiness is present, and vice versa. It's like the rose and the garbage. Without the garbage, there can be no rose. If there is no rose, there can be no garbage. If you have the know-how, you can transform garbage into roses. If you don't have the know-how, the rose quickly turns into garbage. It's a matter of skill. Skill is connected to mindfulness. By speaking, listening, communicating, observing, and acting mindfully, you become skilled at mindful living.

CONCENTRATION IS THE BATTERY; MINDFULNESS IS THE FLASHLIGHT

The practice of stopping brings concentration. Concentration makes our mindfulness more stable. If the battery in our flashlight is fully charged, the light will be strong and stable. We'll be able to see any object we shine it on clearly. But if the battery is weak, we'll only see a vague, flickering image. Concentration is the battery; the flashlight is mindfulness. When we stop and concentrate our minds even a little, we begin to see. If we stop for longer, the energy of concentration in us becomes very strong, and wherever we shine the light of our mindfulness, we can see clearly.

STOP TO LIVE
AUTHENTICALLY

We can practice concentration and looking deeply during all the activities of our daily life. Even while walking, we can practice stopping. We walk in a way that doesn't make arriving the only goal. We walk to enjoy each step. If we practice stopping while sweeping the floor, washing the dishes, or taking a shower, we're living deeply. If we don't practice this way, the days and months will go by as wasted time. Stopping helps us live authentically.

YOU'RE THE MASTER
OF YOURSELF

Walking mindfully is possible anywhere you are.
When you walk, focus all your attention on the act
of walking. Become aware of every step you take and
don't think of anything else. This is called mindful
walking. It's wonderfully effective. By doing this, you
will begin to walk in such a way that every step brings
you solidity, freedom, and dignity. You're the master
of your own self.

THE WISH TO BE HAPPY

The real purpose of walking meditation is to enjoy the walking—walking not to arrive but just to walk, to be in the present moment and enjoy each step. Therefore, you have to shake off all worries and anxieties, not thinking of the future, not thinking of the past, just enjoying the present moment. Anyone can do it. It takes only a little time, a little mindfulness, and the wish to be happy.

EACH STEP IS LIFE

According to the Buddha, life is only available in the
here and now. The past is already gone, and the future
is yet to come. There is only one moment for me to
live—the present moment. So the first thing I do is go
back to the present moment. By doing so, I touch life
deeply. My in-breath is life; my out-breath is life. Each
step I take is life. The air I breathe is life. I can touch
the blue sky and the vegetation. I can hear the sound of
the birds and the sound of another human being. If we
can return to the here and now, we'll be able to touch
the many wonders of life that are available.

ARRIVE 100 PERCENT

If you're new to the practice, you may like to try slow walking meditation. Breathing in, you make just one step, and you say, "I have arrived." Invest all your mind and body into the step and try to arrive 100 percent in the here and now. If you have not arrived 100 percent, you might have arrived only 20 or 25 percent. In that case, don't make another step. Stand there, breathe out, and breathe in again. Challenge yourself to arrive 100 percent in the here and now. Then you smile the smile of victory. You make another step and say, "I am home. I have arrived; I am home." My home is right here in the present moment.

A REAL STEP

Every time we take a step, we know for ourselves if
that step is peaceful, joyful, and solid. You don't need
a teacher to tell you. You know whether your step
has solidity and freedom. If your step doesn't have
freedom, you know it doesn't. If your step doesn't
have solidity, you know it doesn't. It's not hard; it's
so obvious.

FOOTPRINTS
ON THE EARTH

We walk all the time, but usually it's more like running. When we walk like that, we print anxiety and sorrow on the earth. We have to walk in a way that we only print peace and serenity on Earth. Every one of us can do that if we want it very much. When we can take one step peacefully, happily, we support the cause of peace and happiness for all humankind.

A LOTUS BLOOMING
UNDER YOUR FOOT

If you're harried or discontented when you walk, and your steps aren't solid, it's because you're still searching for something in the past or in the future. You aren't aware that what you're searching for is already there in the present moment. If each step you make brings you back to the present, then that step will become as solid as Mother Earth herself. If you make a step like that, it's as though a lotus is blooming under your foot. You walk in freedom, peace, and contentment. You will be one of the most beautiful people on Earth, thanks to your ability to dwell peacefully in the now.

RADIO NST

When you walk, give 100 percent of your awareness and attention to your walking. Don't think about anything else. Most of us have a radio constantly playing in our head tuned to the station Radio NST (Radio Nonstop Thinking). Most of this thinking is unproductive thinking. The more we think, the less available we are to what is around us. Therefore we have to learn to turn off the radio and stop our thinking to fully enjoy the present moment.

PLACING A SEAL ON
THE GROUND

Perhaps you have used a seal before. When you stamp
a seal onto a piece of paper, you make sure that the
whole seal prints on the paper. Then when you remove
the seal, the image is perfect. you remove the seal, the
image is perfect. When we practice walking, we do the
same thing. Every step we take is like placing a seal
on the ground. Mindfulness is the ink. We print our
solidity and peace on the ground. In our daily lives, we
don't usually walk like that. We print our hurry, worry,
depression, and anger on the ground. But now, we
print our solidity, peace, and freedom on the ground.
You know whether you succeed or not with each step.

WE KNOW HOW
TO BE ALIVE

I always tell my friends that they don't have to die to
enter the Kingdom of God—in fact, they have to be
alive to do so. We know how to be alive. Breathing in
and out mindfully, becoming fully present with body
and mind united—these are the conditions for entering
the Kingdom of God. You need only take one step, and
you're there.

SIGN A TREATY
WITH THE ROAD

If there is a set of stairs in your house, sign an agreement with it. Commit yourself to going up and down those stairs in mindfulness and train yourself to enjoy every step. If you take the bus to work, sign a treaty with the road leading from your house to the bus stop. Vow to walk to the bus stop with mindful steps. It doesn't have to be a long path; forty or fifty steps is enough.

"NOW" AND "HERE"

We can use the words "now" and "here" as meditation words. We take a step and say "now." We don't just say the word; we have to be in touch with the now. When we're satisfied, we can take another step and say "here." Only when we're able to be truly in touch, deeply and stably, do we take the next step. During those steps, our mind is completely under our observation. The rope of the mind is tied properly, and it's very pleasant. We can walk alone in an oak grove or along a busy street. We can practice all we want. With each step like that, we step into reality and not a dream.

IN REVERENCE

When we do walking meditation, we can take each
step in gratitude and joy because we know that we're
walking on Mother Earth. We can walk with gentle
steps in reverence to the earth who gave us life and of
whom we're a part. We're aware that the earth we're
walking on is sacred. If we walk like this, every step will
be healing, every step will be nourishing. Walk with
reverence. That is something we can train ourselves to
do. Wherever we walk—in the railway station or the
supermarket—becomes a holy sanctuary.

SOMETHING VERY SPECIAL

Some people possess something very special: they have the now in their heart. Whenever we have a chance to walk alongside such a person, we can feel this subtle source of peace and joy. Their steps are peaceful and free, and that helps us walk with peace and freedom.

You too can walk like this. Walk as if you don't need to get anywhere—as if you're arriving with every step. Each step can bring you back to the wonderful present moment, back to the now.

OUR TRUE HOME IS IN
OUR FEET

Our true home is in our feet. We must walk in such a way that every step helps us touch our true home. Whether we walk in France, Mexico, Botswana, or Canada, we always feel at home. It depends on us and not the place around us.

SURRENDER YOURSELF TO
MOTHER EARTH

When we feel that we're fragile, not stable or solid, we can come back to ourselves and take refuge in the earth. With each step we can feel her solidity beneath our feet. When we're truly in touch with the earth, we can feel her supportive embrace and her stability. We use our whole body and mind to go back to the earth and surrender ourselves to her. With each breath we release all our agitation, our fragility, and our suffering. Just being aware of her benevolent presence can already bring relief.

WALKING WITHOUT
THINKING

While we practice walking meditation, we don't speak; we don't even think. Stop thinking. Maybe you think it's difficult to do, but if you know the way, it's easy. You know that thinking will carry you away to what happened in the past and to what might happen next. Try to be totally in touch with the contact between your feet and the ground. In this way, you see things around you more deeply. You don't need to run away.

WALKING IN THE KINGDOM OF GOD

There isn't a day I don't walk in the Kingdom of God. Wherever I am, I'm always capable of walking mindfully, and the ground beneath my feet is always the Pure Land of the Buddha. No one can take that away from me. For me, the Kingdom of God is now or never. It isn't situated in time or space; it's in our hearts. You have to develop mindful walking and touch the earth as if it's a miracle. If you know how to go back to the here and now, how to touch the Kingdom of God in every cell of your body, the Kingdom will manifest right away.

LIFE, NOT WORK

Thinking that work is one thing and life is another thing is dualistic thinking. For example, after you park your car in the parking lot and begin to walk to your office, you can choose between mindful walking or walking just to arrive at your office. If you know how to walk mindfully, then every step from the parking lot to your office can bring you joy and happiness. You can release the tension in your body and touch the wonders of life with every step. Walking this way is a pleasure. On one hand, you see walking as life; on the other hand, you see walking as labor, as work.

MAINTAINING OUR
FLOWERNESS

Just by breathing in and out and smiling, we have a
flower to offer. The more we practice breathing and
smiling, the more beautiful our flower will become.
A flower doesn't have to do anything to be of service;
it only has to be a flower. That is enough. Being truly
there is enough to make the whole world rejoice. So
please practice breathing in and out and recover your
flowerness. You do it for all of us. Your freshness and
your joy bring us peace.

NO MATTER WHAT

The practice of mindfulness is an art. We train ourselves to be able to generate a feeling of joy and happiness at any time, no matter what the situation. We learn to see that mindfulness is a source of happiness because it helps us to be in touch with the many wonders of life. With mindfulness, we also learn to handle and take care of painful feelings and strong emotions. But we must first learn to generate a feeling of joy and happiness to be strong enough to handle the suffering inside.

LIGHT UP THE LAMP OF
HAPPINESS

When we learn to generate a feeling of happiness,
we create happiness both for ourselves and for other
people. It is contagious. By cultivating happiness, we
remind people around us to be happy. We remind them
that they are in a wonderful world, that the wonders of
life are available to them, and that makes them happy.
We light up the lamp of happiness in them.

THE JOY AND BLISS OF
MEDITATION

The joy and bliss of meditation sustain us. "Experiencing joy, I breathe in. Experiencing joy, I breathe out." This should not be an ideal or wishful thinking; it's a real practice. The Buddha told us that we need to produce joy, beauty, bliss, and happiness to nourish ourselves. We need certain conditions to produce true joy and true happiness. If we don't have joy and happiness, then just saying the words, "Experiencing joy, I breathe in" won't mean anything. We will sit here stiffly, without joy. We have to learn the art of generating joy mindfully, with concentration and insight.

WONDERFUL SEEDS

There are many wholesome, positive seeds deep in our consciousness. If we know how to touch these seeds and water them, they will manifest on the upper level of our consciousness—the mind consciousness. We have to practice looking deeply to recognize our wonderful seeds.

THE SEED OF LOVE

With practice and a friend's support, we can touch our seeds of love, forgiveness, compassion, and joy. Some people say, "I don't know what joy is. I have absolutely no joy within me." That is because that person has not been able to touch the seed of joy within. The practice is to touch it and recognize it. This is the practice of cultivating joy.

OBSTACLES

There are many things we're unable to leave behind
that trap us. Practice looking deeply into these things.
At first, you may think that they're vital to your
happiness, but they may actually be obstacles to your
true happiness and cause you to suffer. If you can't be
happy because you're caught by these things, leaving
them behind will be a source of joy for you. The
Buddha and many of his disciples experienced this and
have handed down their wisdom to us. Please examine
the things you think are necessary to your well-being
and happiness. Find out whether they bring you happiness or are almost killing you.

SKILLFUL WEAVING

We have to touch both the healthy and the ailing parts of our body and consciousness to really touch the truth. The truth will help us be happy and joyful. We have to embrace the unhealthy parts tenderly and mindfully, weaving them into the fabric of our otherwise healthy bodies and minds.

WHAT'S NOT WRONG

Generally, we pay too much attention to what's wrong and not enough attention to what's right. You might ask a friend to tell you what isn't wrong with you. This is important. You should enjoy the positive elements within your body and consciousness.

SMILE TO YOURSELF

There are times when your joy makes you smile. There are also times when a smile causes relaxation, calm, and joy. I don't wait until there's joy in me to smile; joy will come later. Sometimes when I'm alone in my room, I practice smiling to myself. I do this to be kind to myself, to take good care of myself, to love myself. I know that if I cannot take care of myself, I cannot take care of anyone else.

MAKE HAPPINESS SHINE

There are times of difficulty and challenge in each person's life. Each of us still has impressions left by those experiences. We can create happiness by bringing those difficult impressions to mind and comparing them with the conditions of happiness we have right now. This makes the happiness shine right away; you can see it more clearly.

WHEREVER YOU GO, YOU WILL JUST FIND YOURSELF

Whenever we wanted to run away and find something else, my teacher would tell us, "Wherever you go, you will just find yourself." We will just meet the difficulties, the loneliness, the sadness, and the suffering we already know. Nothing is as effective as sitting there, returning to ourselves, and finding the elements of happiness and liberation right here in our own body and mind.

BEAUTIFUL AS YOU ARE

Your body is a kind of flower, and flowers differ from one another. Breathing in, I see myself as a flower. Breathing out, I feel fresh. If you can accept your body, then you have a chance to see your body as a home. If you don't accept your body, you cannot have a home. If you cannot accept your mind, you cannot be a home to yourself. And there are many young people who don't accept their body, who don't accept who they are; they want to be someone else. We have to tell young people that they are already beautiful as they are. They don't have to be another person.

YOUR FLOWER

I have written a calligraphy: "Be beautiful; be yourself."
That is a very important practice. You have to accept
yourself as you are. And when you practice building
a home in yourself, you'll become more and more
beautiful. You have peace, you have warmth, you have
joy. You feel wonderful within yourself. And people
will recognize the beauty of your flower.

LIVING IN THE SPIRIT OF GRATITUDE

Just by practicing gratitude, we can find happiness. We must be grateful to our ancestors, our parents, our teachers, our friends, the earth, the sky, the trees, the grass, the animals, the soil, the stones. Looking at the sunlight or at the forest, we feel gratitude. Looking at our breakfast, we feel gratitude. When we live in the spirit of gratitude, there will be much happiness in our life.

YOU ARE ENLIGHTENED

We run after the Buddha; we run after enlightenment. You don't need to run after enlightenment. You are already enlightened. Wherever you are, steadily there, peaceful, clear in your mind, you are already what you're searching for.

SEEING CLEARLY
AND JOYFULLY

In the northeast United States, the fall foliage of the forests is beautiful. People visit this region just to see the leaves, like a pilgrimage. But the beauty that is perceived and the extent of each person's joy depends on their freedom and peace of mind. If someone's heart is at peace and their mindfulness is strong, their enjoyment of the foliage will be a thousand times greater than that of someone who is suffering and can see only the sorrow of their life. Each person can be looking at the same scenery, but they don't enjoy the same peace and happiness. The difference is their capacity for mindfulness.

A NEW PATH

If you have depression, if you have a problem with your mental health, then the practice of mindfulness, concentration, and insight will help stop you from traveling the same old neural pathways. You open a new path, a path of happiness. Focusing on your suffering isn't the only way to heal. Instead, you focus on the non-suffering side that is in the here and the now.

TRANSFORMATION
AT THE BASE

The roots of our suffering and ignorance can all be found in our store consciousness. For transformation to take place, we shine the light of mindfulness and allow it to penetrate the blocks of pain and delusion that lie in the depths of our consciousness. The secret to transformation at the base is handling the present moment well.

HOW TO LIVE

There are always enough internal and external conditions to make us happy in the present moment. This isn't to deny that there are also elements of suffering in us and around us. But the elements of suffering don't remove the elements of happiness. If we touch only the elements of suffering, we aren't really living.

EMBRACING IT ALL

Some people become imprisoned in their suffering. Wherever they look, they see what is wrong, what is hurtful. They may know in principle that the flower is beautiful, and the sunset is majestic, but they aren't able to touch them. There's a wall surrounding them that prevents them from being in contact with the flower, the sunset, and all the wonders of the natural world that are always available. If these people could touch the healthy and beautiful things that lie within them and around them, their suffering would decrease. It isn't enough to touch our suffering. We have to be in touch with the healthy and wonderful things in life as well.

FREEDOM IS OUR PRACTICE

Freedom is our practice, because every minute the practice can help bring freedom to us—freedom from forgetfulness. We forget that life is a wonder. To be alive, to be present on this planet—full of life, full of wonders—is happiness.

FREEDOM FROM
AFFLICTION

Sometimes our intellect recognizes that the wonders of life are here and now, and yet we cannot get in touch with them because of our anger, our depression, our uncertainty, our despair. And that is what freedom is: freedom from our afflictions. The practice is to get in touch. And the practice of mindfulness is a very concrete way to go home to the here and now and get in touch.

ACCUMULATING PEACE

The purpose of practice is to become free, and with your freedom, happiness is possible. With your freedom and happiness, you can help so many people; you have something to offer them. You don't share your ideas or what you have accumulated from your Buddhist studies. Though Buddhist studies may be helpful, our happiness is the accumulation of peace, and not what we study or the authority we're given in society. Many people in our society aren't truly happy. Our way should be different— it's the way of freedom.

HAPPINESS IS THE WAY

There is no way to happiness; happiness is the way.
Happiness should be found in every moment of your
daily life and not at the end of the road. Life is now,
in every second, in every moment. Peace is every step;
happiness is every step. It's so clear and simple.

THINKING SKILLFULLY

If you want to think in a way that brings more happiness, then you have to be skillfully in touch with the present moment, skillfully in touch with what is positive and wonderful. Don't feel suffocated, suppressed, and miserable. Try to be in touch with what's wonderful inside you, outside you, and around you.

THE TWO FUNCTIONS
OF MINDFULNESS

Mindfulness has two functions. The first is to get in touch with the wonderful and beautiful things all around us. The second is to get in touch with difficult emotions like anger, fear, pain, and sorrow. Mindfulness can help us recognize and embrace these difficulties and transform them. Not only is paradise available in the here and now, but hell is also available. Mindfulness practice helps us to get in touch with both—the wonders, in order to be nourished, and the suffering, in order to heal and transform ourselves.

THE DOOR OF COMMUNICATION

To meditate is to look deeply into the nature of things, including our own nature and the nature of the person in front of us. When we see the true nature of that person, we discover their difficulties, aspirations, suffering, and anxieties. We can sit down, hold our partner's hand, look deeply at them, and say, "Darling, do I understand you enough? Do I water your seeds of suffering? Do I water your seeds of joy? Please tell me how I can love you better." If we say this from the bottom of our heart, they may begin to cry, and that is a good sign. It means the door of communication may be opening again.

MINDFUL LISTENING

If you're mindful and present, the quality of your listening will be good. We call this empathetic, mindful, deep, or compassionate listening. You are willing to help the other person. You know that they suffer deeply, and you may be the first person who has been willing to listen to them. If you are obsessed with your own problems—pulled into the past or sucked into the future—you cannot really be there for the person who needs your help. Mindful listening is an important practice that can relieve a lot of suffering.

EVERY MOMENT CAN BE A
HAPPY MOMENT

When I'm mindful, I enjoy everything more—from my first sip of tea to my first step outside. I'm fully present in the here and now, not carried away by my sorrows, my fears, my projects, the past, or the future. I'm here, available to life. Then life is available to me. Every moment can be a happy moment. You can set an example for others by being mindful yourself, generating awareness and happiness. This will help others do the same for themselves.

ELEGANT SILENCE

You don't need to talk to communicate. If you sit and radiate peace, stability, and joy, you are offering something very precious to the other person. If the other person is truly present and sitting with solidity and peace, you can receive a lot of energy from them. True communication is possible in silence. Silence can be very elegant.

WE'RE IN A
WONDERFUL WORLD

We can create joy and happiness not only for
ourselves but also for other people. Your mindfulness
reminds others to be mindful—it can be contagious.
You remind them that we're in a wonderful world
and that they can touch the wonders of life that are
available. This can make them happy. If you're joyful,
happy, and aware, you light up the lamp of happiness
and joy in others. This is possible because there is a
seed of mindfulness in each of us. It's an art, and it's
not difficult.

BLAMELESS LANGUAGE

The practices of loving speech and compassionate listening are crucial for generating reconciliation and deep, true communication. In our relationships, we and our beloved one may still have wrong perceptions. If we cannot communicate, we can't help each other remove these wrong perceptions. When we use loving speech, we can better communicate our insights and ideas to the other person. We can tell them everything in our heart. The other person needs to understand us better, so we must use the kind of language they can accept, language that has no blame, no accusation. We have the duty to tell them what is in our heart without being judgmental or bitter.

PROTECT YOURSELF
WITH COMPASSION

If you are inhabited by the energy of compassion, you live in the safest of environments. Compassion can be expressed in your eyes, in the way you act or react, in the way you walk, sit, eat, or relate to other people. It's the best means of self-protection, and it can be contagious. It's very wonderful to sit close to someone who has compassion in their heart. With compassion in your heart, you'll win over a friend or two because we all need compassion and love.

UNDERSTANDING MAKES
COMPASSION POSSIBLE

Understanding is the substance out of which we fabricate compassion. What kind of understanding am I talking about? It's the understanding that the other person suffers, too. When we suffer, we tend to believe that we're the victims of other people, that we're the only ones who suffer. That isn't true—the other person also suffers. They have their difficulties, their fears, and their worries, too. If we could only see the pain within them, we would begin to understand them. Once understanding is present, compassion becomes possible.

THE ENERGY OF
THE DHARMA

When you receive the energy of the Dharma from another person, you also radiate it from within yourself. You are also capable of breathing in and out and smiling. Doing this unites your body and mind and brings you to the present moment. That is already the Dharma. You can touch life from within and outside of yourself. That is already enlightenment and awakening. If your smile is born from that kind of awareness and awakening, your smile is the living Dharma. You can generate the living Dharma at any time of the day.

WATERING COLLECTIVE
INTENTION

Within you there is the intention to help, to love, to
protect, and it needs to be watered. Practicing together,
we can help each other nourish this intention. You
acknowledge the existence of the intention to love,
to forgive, to protect in your friend, your loved one.
And when you water the seeds of understanding and
compassion in the other person, you water those seeds
in you; that is a deep practice.

MINDFUL CONVERSATION

Mindful conversation is our practice. When we speak, we should know how that conversation will affect us and other people. If we practice mindfulness of speech, then we'll know whether our conversation is watering our good seeds or the seeds of suffering. With that mindfulness, we can intervene, saying: "Dear friend, let us be aware that talking like this is watering the negative seeds in both of us. It's not healthy. Let us try to talk about things that can bring more hope and joy." This is always possible.

COMMUNICATION
AND LIGHT

When we use loving speech, we avoid misunderstanding and much suffering. Even if other people use harsh language when talking to us, we'll suffer less if we use only loving speech in return. When we have understanding and compassion, we can communicate well with other people, even those who are violent and cruel. We can accept them; we know they are unhappy and victims of their own anger, violence, and discrimination. When compassion and understanding are in us, we're no longer motivated by the desire for punishment or revenge. Loving speech becomes available to us, and communication becomes possible.

RETURNING HOME

Can your family come home to itself? You don't need
to wait until you have transformed all your suffering to
help your family. Use loving speech and listen deeply
in communication with your parents, your partner, and
your children. Persuade them to join you on the path of
transformation and healing because your family should
be the foundation of support for your practice.

REBUILDING OUR FAMILY

There are families where nobody feels familial. The home is like a hotel where people simply go to sleep; everyone has their own life, and there is no communication, no mutual support. The practice of returning home to ourselves rebuilds the family and turns it into an organism.

TELEVISION MEDITATION

We can discuss with our children how to watch television intelligently so that their negative seeds aren't watered. If your child watches a television program full of violence, craving, and fear—even if they are excited by the events shown in the film—they will be tired after an hour. You may like to talk to them then. Say that you have something to discuss with them and propose that they turn off the television. Ask if they feel peaceful and happy after watching such a film. They will tell you the truth. Then you can discuss an intelligent strategy for using the television set. There are many healthy programs available.

RELAXING WITH
THE FAMILY

If there is a pleasant path in your backyard or in your neighborhood, you can turn walking meditation into a delight for the whole family. You may combine a picnic with walking meditation and total relaxation on the grass.

We can do five minutes of total relaxation in our home every day. To do this, we lie down, and someone guides us in releasing all our muscles. We practice breathing and smiling for five or ten minutes. At first, we might like to use a recording; later each member of the family can take turns offering total relaxation. This is the kind of nourishment we really need. If we do one session of total relaxation a day, we'll be free from stress.

A BUDDHA IS IN EVERY
ONE OF US

Someone who is awake, who knows, who understands, is called a buddha. A buddha is in every one of us. We can become awake, understanding, and loving. I often tell children that if their mother or father is very understanding and loving, if they smile and are lovely like a flower while they take care of the family, the child can say, "Mommy, Daddy, you're a buddha today."

THE CAPACITY TO
TAKE CARE

Love is the capacity to take care, protect, and nourish. If you aren't able to generate that kind of energy toward yourself, it's very difficult to take care of another person.

LOVING OURSELVES

We need to learn to love ourselves, to be fully present and at peace with ourselves. So, our mindfulness always begins with ourselves. When we practice like this, our very smile and our conscious breathing contribute to creating a calm, caring, and solid community.

FEELING AT HOME
ANYWHERE

Sometimes we feel that we aren't in our true home because the person we love isn't there. We think that if we can be together with our beloved, we'll feel more at home. But if we have not found our true home, then even when we're with the person we love, we won't feel at home. This is why it's very important for us to find our true home first. Only then can we help our beloved one find their true home. Otherwise, both of us will be without a home, still looking somewhere outside of ourselves.

We should not think that our true home is wherever our beloved one is. Our true home is in our heart. And when we have found our true home, we feel at home anywhere we go.

TOGETHER WE'RE HAPPY

When we look deeply into others, we're looking deeply into ourselves at the same time. If we think the other person is someone other than us, that their success or failure has nothing to do with us, then we have not been successful in our looking deeply. The happiness of that person is linked to our own happiness. If we're not happy, the other person can't be happy, and our larger community won't be happy.

REAL LOVE

When you first fall in love and feel attached to the other person, that isn't yet real love. Real love means loving kindness and compassion, the kind of love that doesn't have any conditions. You form a community of two to practice love—taking care of each other, helping your partner blossom, and making happiness something real in that small community.

THE ART OF MAKING
ONE PERSON HAPPY

By learning the art of making one person happy, you learn to express your love for the whole of humanity and all beings.

MAKING SPACE

When you love someone, you don't impose your ideas on them and deprive them of their freedom. You offer them space both inside and outside. Often, we make our love a prison. We lock up our beloved, and they can no longer be themselves. This is a kind of dictatorship, where spaciousness isn't present. We have to go to them and say, "Darling, have I deprived you of your freedom? Do you still feel that you can be yourself? Do you have enough space inside and around you? Have I deprived you of that space?" If you ask sincerely, they will tell you. If they still feel free, you know that it's true love.

THE GREATEST LOVE

When a parent loves their child, they should not say, "I have given you everything, yet you don't respond. You behave badly." That isn't equanimity. When you give in the spirit of equanimity, you give something of the greatest value. When you love in the spirit of equanimity, that is the greatest love. You don't expect love in return. That would not be true love. Many of us don't know much about how to love; we have a lot to learn. That is why love can make us suffer.

BRING THEM BACK TO LIFE

When you're really present, you can recognize the presence of your beloved. To be loved means to be recognized as existing. It's very simple. When you're driving, you might think about everything except the person sitting by your side. You might completely ignore them. Your forgetfulness—not your presence or mindfulness—embraces them. A person who is ignored, whose presence isn't acknowledged, slowly dies. Only mindfulness can bring them back to life. That is why when you're really present, you can look at your beloved and declare, "Darling, I know you are there, and I am very happy." Embraced by your mindfulness, your beloved will bloom like a flower.

REVERENCE IS THE NATURE
OF OUR LOVE

What happens in the body will affect the mind and vice versa. When you love someone, you have to respect not only their mind but also their body. You respect your own body, and you respect their body. True love should have the nature of reverence, of respect. In the Asian tradition you have to treat your partner with respect, like an honored guest. And to respect them, you have to respect yourself first. Reverence should be the nature of our love.

THICH NHAT HANH

TRUE RELIEF

Even if you have a so-called healthy self, you will
continue to suffer if you're trapped in the idea of a self.
True relief comes when you're free from the notion
of self. If your notion of self is strong and you're in a
relationship, you know what will happen: there will be
a clash between self and self. When we give ourselves
up and become one with our beloved, we're practicing
nonself. Our degree of happiness, understanding, and
love increases a thousandfold.

ARE YOU CAPABLE
OF GIVING?

You don't have to go to the store to buy your beloved a gift. There are many gifts that you can give right now—a smile, a loving look. Are you capable of giving? Can you give your joy, your stability, and your freedom? Breathing in, you know that you're alive and that your beloved is alive in front of you. With this insight, you smile beautifully, and your anger disappears. That smile, that joy, that capacity to cherish your own and your beloved's presence is a great gift.

If someone has made us suffer, it's because that person is also suffering. Someone who doesn't know how to handle their suffering will allow it to spill over, and we'll become a victim of their suffering. We know that someone who suffers that much needs help and not punishment. When we begin to see that, compassion is born, and we don't suffer anymore. Compassion is an antidote for anger. Once we're motivated by the desire to help the other person suffer less, we're free from our anger.

SELECTIVE WATERING

We can water positive seeds of happiness, loving kindness, forgiveness, and joy in the other person. We call this the practice of selective watering. We water the flowers, not the garbage, so that the flowers will bloom in the other person. Flower watering should be authentic and based on the truth. When you see the positive seed in the other person, you express it: "Darling, I see a wonderful seed in you. That seed can bring you and many people happiness." If they don't practice, they don't know that the seed is in them. You can help them to water it. You recognize the seed and tell them that it's very precious. When we make the other person smile, we benefit as well. It doesn't take long to see the result of our practice.

WATERING GOOD SEEDS
EVERY DAY

Arrange things in your daily life so that you have time to water your positive seeds. Ask your loved ones to practice in the same way. Say, "Darling, if you really care for me, please water the good seeds in me every day. I am capable of loving, understanding, and forgiving, and I need your help to practice these in my daily life. I promise to recognize the positive seeds in you as well, and to do my best to water them every day." This is true love.

PREPARING A GIFT

When you're angry at someone, try giving them a
present. When you aren't angry at the other person,
prepare the present. Wrap it with loving kindness,
with all your heart. Think, "I'm preparing this gift for
them. My heart is full of love and the desire to make
my beloved happy. In the future, I may be angry at
my beloved, and I resolve to send them this gift then."
You do this with the awareness that your love is imper-
manent. The gift that you're preparing may one day
restore your love. When you're angry at them, go to
the post office and mail it. You will feel much better.

MEDITATION IN DAILY LIFE

If you're aware of what is going on, then you can see
problems as they unfold, and you can help prevent
many of them. When things explode, it's too late.
How we deal with our daily lives is the most important
question. How we deal with our feelings, our speaking,
with ordinary things every day is meditation. We must
learn to apply meditation in our daily lives.

SHARING YOUR
ASPIRATION

You should be able to share your concerns, your aspirations, and your difficulties with your partner and your family so that all of you become stronger. If you don't include your partner in your mindfulness, they become an obstacle. And you become an obstacle for them. When you have the support of your family and good communication, you no longer feel lonely, and you have plenty of happiness. Then you have the energy to pursue your dreams.

BEAUTY AND FRESHNESS

When you arrange flowers, it's good to leave space
around each flower so it can reveal itself in its full
beauty and freshness. You don't need a lot of flowers—
two or three are enough. We human beings also need
space to be happy. We practice stopping and becoming
calm to offer space to ourselves, inside and outside,
and to those we love. We need to let go of our projects,
preoccupations, worries, and regrets to create space
around us. Space is freedom.

LOVE WITHOUT LIMITS

When we know how to nourish our love, we can heal ourselves and those around us. When love grows, it naturally embraces more and more. If your love is true love, then it will continue to grow until it includes all people and all species. Your love will become a river, wide enough to nourish not only you and your beloved but the whole world. This is love without limits, a heart without boundaries and discrimination.

TRANSFORMING OUR SITUATION

Our daily lives, the way we drink, what we eat, have to do with the world's political situation. Meditation is looking deeply into things, seeing how we can change, how we can transform our situation.

THE REAL MEANING OF
ENGAGED BUDDHISM

By transforming our situation, we transform our minds; by transforming our minds, we transform our situation. The situation is mind, and mind is situation. Awakening is important. The nature of bombs, the nature of injustice, the nature of weapons, and the nature of our own being are the same. This is the real meaning of Engaged Buddhism.

THICH NHAT HANH

JUSTICE BEGINS WITH US

Peace, social justice, and equality should begin with us. We have to learn to deal with ourselves with compassion. We have to learn how to be understanding with our parents and our siblings before we can help another family do the same. Although we may have a perfect analysis of the situation and a very thorough plan of action, without this kind of training or practice, without a spiritual dimension, we can't succeed.

REAL EMANCIPATION

Many people embrace Buddhism because they believe
that Buddhism offers a chance for social change
and social justice. But it's the basic practice of daily
mindfulness that will bring about real emancipation.
Political action isn't enough; social action isn't enough.
There has to be real, solid mindfulness practice along
with it. Political and social change will be possible, will
be much easier, when we have that foundation of spiritual practice.

You can only serve the cause of transformation and healing if you have practiced transformation and healing within yourself. You can only serve the cause of peace when you have some peace within yourself. It's as simple as that.

THE ENERGY OF
THE BUDDHA

Every time you achieve transformation and healing,
you know that it's for the benefit of many. Practice
cultivating the energy of the Buddha in yourself
and touch it every day, not as a vague concept or
an abstraction, but as the energy of mindfulness.
This energy will act as a source of light to guide and
nourish you.

Can the peace movement show the way for peace? I think that will depend on whether the people in the peace movement can be peace. Because without being peace, we cannot do anything for peace. If we cannot smile, we cannot help other people to smile. If we aren't peaceful, then we cannot contribute to the peace movement.

ACTS OF PEACE

Every time we breathe in and go home to ourselves,
creating internal harmony and joy, we're performing
an act of peace. Every time we look at other people
and recognize the suffering that has led them to speak
or act unskillfully, every time we can see that they're
victims of their suffering, our heart of compassion
grows. When we can look at other people with the
eyes of understanding and love, we don't suffer, and we
don't make other people suffer. These are the actions
of peace that can be shared with other people.

NON-ACTION

Sometimes if we don't do anything, we help more than if we do a lot. We call that non-action. It's like the calm person on a small boat in a storm. That person doesn't have to do much, just be themself, and the situation can change.

"DON'T JUST DO SOMETHING: SIT THERE"

Stopping is also seeing, and seeing helps stopping. The two are one. We do so much, we run so quickly, the situation is difficult, and many people say, "Don't just sit there, do something." But doing more may make the situation worse. So you should say, "Don't just do something: sit there." But you have to really sit.

GETTING IN TOUCH
WITH SUFFERING

Much of the suffering in the West is unnecessary. It can vanish when we see the real suffering of other people. Sometimes we suffer because of some psychological fact. We cannot get out of ourself, and so we suffer. If we get in touch with the suffering in the world and are moved by that suffering, we may come forward to help the people who are suffering, and our own suffering may just vanish.

REAL HAPPINESS

Our life will be filled with happiness if we can help others around us. But if we spend our whole life building up our name and our fortune, we cannot find happiness. We might have a lot of money, a big house, and a luxurious car, but that's not real happiness. We can only taste real happiness when we can help others.

UNDERSTANDING
AND LOVE

To develop understanding, you have to practice looking at all living beings with the eyes of compassion. When you understand, you love. And when you love, you naturally act in a way that can relieve people's suffering.

NO LONGER A SMALL "SELF"

As you continue practicing, the flower of insight will blossom in you, along with the flowers of compassion, tolerance, happiness, and letting go. You can let go because you don't need to keep anything for yourself. You're no longer a fragile and small "self" that needs to be preserved by all possible means. Since the happiness of others is also your happiness, you're now filled with joy, and you have no jealousy or selfishness. Free from attachment to wrong views and prejudices, you're filled with tolerance. The door of your compassion is wide open, and you also suffer the sufferings of all living beings. As a result, you do whatever you can to relieve these sufferings.

THE PARADOX OF GENEROSITY

There's a kind of vegetable in Vietnam called *he* (pronounced "hey"). It belongs to the onion family and looks like a scallion; it's very good in soup. The more you cut the plants at the base, the more they grow. If you don't cut them, they won't grow very much, but if you cut them often, right at the base of the stalk, they grow bigger and bigger.

This is also true of the practice of generosity. If you give and continue to give, you become richer and richer all the time, richer in terms of happiness and well-being. This may seem strange, but it's always true.

GIVING IS THE FOUNDATION
OF YOUR WELL-BEING

The more you give away the things that you value—not just material things but also gifts of time and energy—the greater your store of riches. How is this possible? When you try to hoard things, you may end up losing them, but everything you give to help others always remains with you as the foundation of your well-being.

THICH NHAT HANH

THE EMPTINESS OF GIVING

True generosity isn't a trade or a bargaining strategy. In true giving, there is no thought of giver and recipient. This is called the "emptiness of giving," in which there is no perception of separation between the one who gives and the one who receives. This is the practice of generosity in the spirit of wisdom. You offer help as naturally as you breathe. You don't see yourself as the giver and the other person as the recipient of your generosity, as someone who is now beholden to you and must be suitably grateful, respond to your demands, and so on. You don't give to make the other person your ally. When you see that people need help, you offer and share what you have with no strings attached and no thought of reward.

SOCIETY WITHIN

Our suffering represents both our individual suffering
and the suffering of our ancestors, parents, and society.
Every time we practice mindful breathing and take
good care of our body and feelings, we relieve some of
our suffering. We get the benefit of the transformation
and healing, and our ancestors and society also get the
benefit. Every smile will affect society. We can touch
society within ourselves.

Any step we take in mindfulness that brings us a little more solidity, freedom, and joy also benefits society and our ancestors. Don't think that what you do to yourself doesn't affect the rest of society and the world. Peace and freedom always begin with our own practice. If transformation takes place in us, it takes place in the world at the same time. If peace is in you, peace becomes possible everywhere in the cosmos.

YOUR BEAUTIFUL
CONTINUATION

Thought, speech, and actions—everything you do in these three aspects continues. And that is your continuation. The Buddhist term is called karma, which means action. If we know how to practice according to the recommendation of the Buddha, with right thinking, right speech, and right action, we're sure to be a beautiful continuation, a happy continuation.

THAT IS PEACE

Are we doing anything to help end the violence? If we allow ourselves to be overwhelmed by feelings of anger and despair, we won't be able to help. We may even add fuel to the situation, increase its intensity, and make it last longer. So the question is whether we can do something for peace—*be* something for peace—right in the present moment. When you think a thought of compassion, loving kindness, understanding—that is peace. When you do something to help victims of war and violence suffer less, such as bringing food to homeless or refugee children, that action can relieve suffering and help end war and violence.

WITH OUR LOVE, WE CAN
DO SOMETHING

We must first accept the situation as it is if we're to find ways to change it. Climate change has come about from the way each of us lives our daily life. If we don't practice forbearance, patience, then we give in to our despair, our anger. And the worst thing that can happen to us is despair. If we're overwhelmed, if we're carried away by despair, anger, violence, there is nothing left; there's no hope. This is why we must practice patience, to bear, to accept. But this isn't a kind of negative, passive acceptance. Because we know that with our understanding, with our love, we can do something. We can always do something to change the situation.

IT ISN'T SOLD IN THE
SUPERMARKET

Some people spend their whole life trying to get
revenge. This kind of desire will bring great suffering
not only to others but to oneself as well. Hatred is a
fire that burns in every soul and can only be tempered
by compassion. But where do we find compassion?
It isn't sold in the supermarket. If it were, we would
only need to bring it home, and we could solve all
the hatred and violence in the world very easily. But
compassion can only be produced in our own heart by
our own practice.

OPENING THE WAY FOR
THE NEXT GENERATION

With mindfulness, we see that the way of life in our society is one of separation, fear, discrimination, and hatred; we want to transform this. We want our civilization to be one of siblinghood, of compassion, a society that can open the way for the next generation. Siblinghood is a powerful source of energy that makes us lucid and able to help build our community and change the situation.

THROW IT INTO
THE FLAMES

We tend to think that anger is the only energy that can push us to act. We may have been holding onto our anger and suffering for a long time, but it hasn't helped us to do anything constructive. It's time to release our anger, throw it into the flames, so we can have a new source of energy.

NO ENEMIES

We sometimes believe, "Until this person or that institution changes, I can't be happy." We may make a particular person or group of people into our enemy; we think they are the obstacle to our happiness. But our suffering comes from our own ignorance and lack of understanding, not from other people. When we understand this, we can open our arms to embrace all peoples, all species, and we have no enemies.

AS LIGHT AS A CLOUD

To have no enemies is such a wonderful thing. When we have no enemies, no reproach, and no blaming, our mind is light as a cloud, and our happiness is immense. We don't look at those who hurt us as our enemies but as people who need understanding and compassion. When we look in this way, we can call ourselves the children of the Buddha, disciples of the Buddha, and no one is our enemy.

THOSE I WANT TO HELP

Even those who have created a lot of suffering and injustice, who have tried to kill or suppress me, they aren't my enemies; they are the ones I want to help. If we practice mindfulness of the present moment, we can transform our mind and our heart and become a bodhisattva—a great being. We can then help others transform, even those we have considered to be oppressors, abusers, those who discriminate against us, who try to suppress us, kill us, and so on. They are also victims of their own ignorance and anger, and they don't know how to handle their strong emotions. This is the path shown to us by the Buddha.

OUR SAFETY

We have to wake up to the fact that everything is connected to everything else. Safety and well-being cannot be individual matters anymore. If another group isn't safe, there is no way that we can be safe. Taking care of their safety is at the same time taking care of our own safety. Taking care of their well-being is taking care of our own well-being. It's the mind of discrimination and separation that is at the foundation of all hate and violence.

MIRACLE OF LOVE

If our heart remains small, we may suffer very deeply from all the difficulties we encounter in life—heat, cold, floods, bacteria, sickness, old age, death, stubborn people, cruel people. But through the practice of inclusiveness, we can embrace everything, and we won't have to suffer. A small heart cannot accept too much—it cannot take in and embrace everything, every difficulty that arises. But a heart that is expansive and open can easily accept everything, and you no longer have to suffer. Perfecting the practice of inclusiveness consists of continually making your heart bigger. That is the power and the miracle of love.

HOW LARGE IS MY HEART?

Each of us must ask ourselves, how large is my heart?
How can I help my heart grow bigger and bigger
every day?

EMBRACING EVERYTHING

The practice of inclusiveness is based on the practice of understanding, compassion, and love. When you practice looking deeply to understand suffering, the nectar of compassion will arise naturally in your heart. Loving kindness and compassion can continue to grow indefinitely. So thanks to the practice of looking deeply and understanding, your loving kindness and compassion grow day by day. And with enough understanding and love, you can embrace and accept everything and everyone.

PEACE AND SECURITY

If we know how to allow the other side into our heart—those who oppose us or think differently than we do—we increase our own chances of having peace and security. When we're motivated by the intention to practice inclusiveness, it becomes very easy to ask, "How can we best help you so that you can enjoy safety? Please tell us." We express our concern for their safety, their need to live in peace, to rebuild their country, to strengthen their society. When you can approach a situation of conflict in this way, it can help transform the situation very quickly. The basis for this transformation, the first thing that must happen, is the change within your own heart. You open your heart to include the other side; you want to give them the opportunity to live in peace, as you wish to live.

INTO THE MARKETPLACE

We can bring the spiritual dimension into our daily
life, as well as our social, political, and economic life.
This is our practice. Jesus had this intention. Buddha
had this intention. All our spiritual ancestors, whether
Christian, Jewish, Muslim, Hindu, or Buddhist had this
intention. We can display the light of wisdom and come
together to create hope and prevent society and the
younger generation from sinking into despair.

BUDDHISM MUST BE ENGAGED

There are so many practices we can do to bring awareness into our everyday lives: breathing between telephone calls, walking meditation between business meetings, practicing meditation while helping hungry children or war victims. Buddhism must be engaged. What is the use of practicing meditation if it doesn't have anything to do with our daily lives?

TOUCHING OUR
TRUE HOME

The expression "I have arrived, I am home" is the embodiment—the cream—of my practice. It expresses my understanding of the Buddha's teaching. Since the time I found my true home, I haven't suffered. The past is no longer a prison for me. The future is no longer a prison for me. I am able to live in the here and now and touch my true home.

THICH NHAT HANH

OUR TRUE HOME
IS RIGHT HERE

Our true home is the place without discrimination, the place without hatred. Our true home is the place where we no longer seek, no longer wish, no longer regret. Our true home isn't the past; it isn't the object of our regrets, our yearning, our longing, or remorse. Our true home isn't the future; it's not the object of our worries, hopes, or fears. Our true home lies right in the present moment. If we can practice according to the teaching of the Buddha and return to right here and right now, then the energy of mindfulness will help us to establish our true home in the present moment.

HELPING OTHERS
TRANSFORM

When we're protected by understanding and compassion, we aren't victims anymore. Others may still be victims of their own ignorance and discrimination. These people are the object of our practice. We live in such a way that we can help them remove and transform their ignorance, discrimination, craving, and hatred.

COMING TOGETHER
WITH OPENNESS

When we return to the present moment to be in touch with our true home, we no longer discriminate and we no longer have a narrow mind. Our mind is vast, our heart is open, and we embrace and learn from every race, every culture. If young people can open their hearts to learn about other cultures, they will find much goodness, beauty, and enrichment. When we can do that ourselves, we can help those who are stuck to understand and accept people from other cultures. Coming together with openness and acceptance, we can transform hatred, and we contribute to preventing war in our own personal way.

THE WISDOM OF
NONDISCRIMINATION

Because many of us have suffered, we may feel that
we're inferior and without value. The teaching of the
Buddha can help us to attain the wisdom of nondiscrimination, which can free us from this inferiority
complex. We may instead have a superiority complex,
thinking that we're better than others. Or, we may have
an equality complex, a desire always to be the same as
everyone else, even when that doesn't make sense for
the situation. According to the teaching of the Buddha,
we cannot compare; there is no self to compare, and
nothing to compare with. The right hand and the left
hand don't have a separate self. When we see that we
can't compare and shouldn't try to, we don't suffer.

THICH NHAT HANH

COLLECTIVE KARMA

We must be aware that we're always in the process of creating our environment with our thoughts, words, and actions. In this way, we contribute to creating our collective environment, our society. For example, suppose we have a political leader or a representative that we don't trust very much. We cannot say that we aren't responsible for this representative; their service is the result of the whole country's collective karma. We should not blame because we have contributed to our current situation. If society is full of violence, fear, and hate, it's partly our collective karma. We have allowed things to become this way. With awakening, enlightenment, and mindfulness, we can change things.

WE CAN BE HOPEFUL

The practice of the Dharma is a collective practice. It is the practice of helping ourselves and others wake up to the fact that we have a beautiful planet, and that we aren't protecting the planet at all. This is why enlightenment is very important. Every one of us has the seed of enlightenment in us. And we can be hopeful—because if people wake up, social change won't take much time. With collective awakening, things can go very quickly. This is why everything we do should aim at helping to bring about collective awakening.

REDUCING VIOLENCE

It's possible to do something every day to reduce the violence in society. When you make a peaceful step, calming your emotions, you're already making a difference.

START TODAY

Everyone can be a buddha if you're inspired by the desire to serve. You can do it, and you can begin today. Every breath, every smile, every step made in mindfulness is an act of peace, decreasing suffering and violence. It will help transform the situation and bring transformation and healing to the people around us.

THE GOOD NEWS

Reading newspapers and watching the news are forms
of consumption. There is so much violence and despair
in the news that we view every day. We must decide
not to water the seeds of violence, fear, and despair
in us. We don't want to be cut off from the world; we
want to know what is going on. But we don't need to
read newspapers and watch television every day. The
positive elements should be reported more. If the
daffodils are coming up, it's not reported. But that is
very good news.

WHAT IS MY DEEPEST
DESIRE IN THIS LIFE?

We have to ask ourselves, "What is my deepest desire in this life?" Our desire can take us in the direction of happiness or in the direction of suffering. Desire is a kind of food that nourishes us and gives us energy. If you have a healthy desire—such as a wish to protect life, protect the environment, or live simply with time to take care of yourself and your beloved ones—your desire will bring you happiness.

Ask yourself, "Where is my desire taking me? What is its nature?"

SOMETHING MORE

If your deepest intention, your desire, is only to make money, to become the number one corporation, that's not enough. There are those who have a lot of money and a lot of power, and yet they aren't happy.

So your desire is not to have a lot of money, to have social recognition, to have a lot of power or fame. What you really want may be something more. Maybe you want to reverse the direction of civilization. You want to help the earth restore her beauty. You want to help people know how to heal and transform, how to generate joy and happiness so that they can help their beloved ones do the same. These are good desires.

A TREMENDOUS SOURCE
OF ENERGY

What do you want to do with your life? That is the question. Of course, you have the right to look for material and affective comforts, but that isn't your deepest desire. Do you have an ultimate concern? Do you know the meaning of your life? That can be a tremendous source of energy.

YOU HAVE TO
REALLY WANT IT

Do you want to live as a free person without worries or craving? The desire to be a free person is very worthwhile. To be free means you're no longer the victim of fear, anger, craving, or suspicion. Do you want this? Maybe you want it, but you don't want it enough. You have other desires that get in the way, such as wanting a bigger house, a better car, or tastier food. Those little desires distract you from your most noble desire. If you want to realize your deep desire, you have to really want it.

ONLY MINDFULNESS

It's wonderful to be alive and walking on Earth. You don't need money and power or fame to do that; you need only mindfulness.

A SIMPLER LIFE

Many in our society can't walk peacefully. They are
so busy. There's a tendency for us to rush. We don't
have time to live. We might have more money than our
ancestors, but we don't have more time. We believe
that time must be used to make money, but time is life.
We need to ask how to live a simpler life so that we can
live more deeply every moment. We have to resist the
tendency to run, to burn up our life.

NO LONGING, NO CRAVING

When we long for something very strongly, when we
crave something very strongly, we lose the present
moment; we lose ourselves and all the wonders of
life available in the present moment. We lose life
itself. And we know that happiness isn't possible
when we're sucked into the future, always desiring
something. We do the following practice: breathing in, I release my longing; I release my craving for
something in the future; breathing out, I contemplate
no longing, no craving.

THICH NHAT HANH

BREAKING FREE

We don't want to live a life of bondage, a life of slavery. We want to be free. Only when we're free can we really be happy. Therefore we want to break out of the prisons that keep us from being free. These prisons are our passion, our infatuation, our hatred, our jealousy. The practitioner is like a deer that gets out of a trap and runs freely in any direction, avoiding all other traps.

BE FREE AND BRING RELIEF

I don't desire wealth. I can be very happy without money or power. Sometimes we think that when we're poor, we can't do anything. That's simply not true. We can help so many people. When we're free, we can do so many things to help our people, our community. It's possible to live simply and happily. When we transform ourselves into a bodhisattva, a great being, we generate a lot of power. It's not the power of fame or wealth. It's the kind of power that helps us to be free and bring relief to many people.

BECOMING OUR
COMMUNITY'S HOPE

With mindful consumption we can find a way out. Many companies want to get rich, so they will produce anything to make money. They create films, music, books, and video games that are full of violence, which can destroy our children. If we know how to boycott these kinds of products, these companies cannot continue. We boycott these items to protect ourselves and our family. We have to come together and discuss a strategy of self-protection, mutual protection. We can become the hope of our community because we're capable of practicing mindful consumption.

WORKING GENTLY,
LIVING SIMPLY

In my community, I bind books. Using a toothbrush, a small wheel, and a very heavy fireproof brick, I can bind two hundred books in a day. I'm at peace while assembling the pages, gluing them, and putting the cover on the book. I know I cannot produce as many books in a day as a professional bookbinder or a machine, but I also know that I don't hate my job. If you want a lot of money to spend, you must work hard and quickly, but if you live simply, you can work gently with full awareness.

THICH NHAT HANH

A PROMISING SIGN

I know many young people who prefer to work less, perhaps four hours a day, earning a small livelihood, so they can live simply and happily. This may be a solution to our society's problems—reducing the production of useless goods, sharing work with those who have none, and living simply and happily. Some individuals and communities have already proved that it's possible. This is a promising sign for the future, isn't it?

THE NEW CULTURE

To be happy, we have to learn to live simply. When we live simply, we have much more time, and we can be in touch with the many wonders of life. Living simply is the criterion for the new culture, the new civilization. With the development of technology, people lead more and more complicated lives. Shopping has replaced other activities as a way to satisfy ourselves. To be happy you must live simply, with harmony and peace in yourself and with the people around you.

KNOW THE LIMIT

We must know the limit, we must know how much is enough. This is the antidote for wanting more and more. You know what is sufficient, what is enough for you.

GOOD ENOUGH IS ENOUGH

"Good enough" means being content with the minimum amount necessary. Your shirt and pair of shoes can last another year. It's all right for three or four people to share a desk; there's no need for each person to have their own. Settling for good enough in terms of simple living will bring us contentment, satisfaction, and happiness immediately. If we think our lives aren't good enough, we won't have happiness. As soon as we realize our lives are good enough, happiness immediately appears. That is the practice of contentment.

DON'T WASTE YOUR LIFE

We should not waste our life. We have wasted a lot of our life; day after day, we practiced running. We were not able to touch the wonders of life deeply for our transformation, our nourishment, our happiness. When we touch life deeply in the here and now, we water the seed of love within ourselves. We know how to take care of ourselves. We know how to smile, how to have compassion for ourselves and for other people. There are seeds of happiness to water every day, and there are seeds of suffering and affliction to be transformed every day.

A CAUSE FOR GREAT
HAPPINESS

There are many lucrative vocations that, because they aren't ethical, keep us twisting and turning in bed at night. Those vocations cause harm to others or to the environment, and they force us to lie and hide the truth. Even though these jobs may be lucrative, they cause us deep suffering. When we can find a job that expresses our ideal of compassion, happiness arises, even if the job isn't as lucrative. Having a vocation that does not cause harm to others or the environment, a job through which we can express our compassion, is a cause for great happiness.

THE SPIRIT OF
TOGETHERNESS

As individuals, we have suffered tremendously.
Individualism is predominating and families are
breaking down. Society has become deeply divided as
a result.

We must be guided by the spirit of togetherness.
We should learn to do things together, to share our
ideas and the deep aspiration in our hearts. We have
to learn to see the Sangha, our community, as our
own body. We need each other to practice solidity,
freedom, and compassion so that we can remind
people that there is always hope.

YOU AREN'T ALONE

Even if you cannot, at first, find others to practice with
you, start practicing mindfulness by yourself. People
are practicing all over the world. You aren't alone.
Every one of us can contribute to the collective energy
of mindfulness. Your practice of mindful breathing and
mindful walking supports us all.

TRUSTING IN SANGHA

When we touch the ground, we can feel the stability of the earth. We can also feel stability in the sunshine, the air, and the trees—we can count on the sun to rise tomorrow and the trees to be there for us. We have to put our trust in what is stable. When we build a house, we build it on solid ground. When we say, "I take refuge in the Sangha," it means we put our trust in a community of solid practitioners. The teacher and the teachings can be important, but friends are the most essential element of the practice. It's difficult—even impossible—to practice without a Sangha.

ALLOW YOURSELF
TO BE HELD

Taking refuge in the Sangha isn't a declaration of faith. It's a practice. It means you allow yourself to be held by the Sangha. You have confidence in the Sangha. Allow yourself to be in a Sangha as a drop of water allows itself to be in a river. The energy of the Sangha can penetrate you, and transformation and healing become possible.

TRANSFORMING
NATURALLY

It's a joy to find ourselves in the midst of a Sangha where people are practicing well together. Each person's way of walking, eating, and smiling can be a real help to us. She is walking for me, I am smiling for her, and we do it together, as a Sangha. By practicing together like this, we can expect a real transformation within us. We don't have to practice intensively or force ourselves. We just have to allow ourselves to be in a good Sangha where people are happy, living deeply each moment, and transformation will come naturally, without much effort.

COLLECTIVE NOURISHMENT

If you can sit in meditation on your own, quietly and
peacefully, that is wonderful. Even if nobody else
knows you're meditating, the energy you produce
is still beneficial. The beautiful, peaceful energy you
create will go out into the world. But if you sit with
others, if you walk and work with others, the energy
you create is amplified. You will have a lot more energy
for your own healing and the healing of the world. It's
too much for one person to do alone! Don't deprive
the world of this essential spiritual food.

THE GREATEST BLESSING

The greatest blessing is to be near good, wise, kindhearted friends. We can't be happy unless we have a sane, healthy space within us and around us. We need a habitat that is beautiful and nourishing, one that gives us the safety and freedom we need.

CREATING CONDITIONS
FOR LASTING HAPPINESS

Our community can be a family that sustains us. We can't handpick everybody with whom we interact in our daily life, but we can choose to live among those who are kind and virtuous. When we can interact with those who are honorable and have great virtue, we're creating conditions that will bring us lasting happiness.

A REMINDER TO LET GO

Have you ever met someone who seems to be skilled in the art of letting go? A friend or a teacher can help us let go of worry, craving, and concern, so we can be free to encounter the wonders of life in the here and now.

UNDISTURBED BY THE EBB
AND FLOW OF LIFE

If we see someone who isn't disturbed by the ebb and
flow of life, not enmeshed in afflictions, that person has
freedom; that person is solid. To be with such a person
is the highest blessing. When we master this quality,
all of our worldly afflictions dissolve, and we become
indestructible, completely at peace. We can become that
person by practicing happiness in the present moment.

COMMUNITIES OF
RESISTANCE

For many years I have been speaking about the need
to create communities of resistance, communities of
mindful living that offer an alternative to the unhealthy
and wasteful ways of living that so many people are
engaged in. We're constantly being exposed to negative
things in society, assaulted day and night by what we
see and hear. The negative seeds in us are watered every
day, and they continue to grow. We have to reflect on
how to organize our families and communities so that
we can be protected from the constant invasion and
assault of craving, hostility, and delusion. If we don't
protect ourselves from the influence of these poisons,
we won't be able to protect others, including our own
children and loved ones.

THE JOY THAT COMES
WITH PRACTICE

If we try to consume mindfully by ourselves, we'll surely fail. There are so many toxins out there; we can't help but see trouble and despair at every turn. In the face of all these negatives, your Sangha is your antidote. It's a place where people can feel safe. The work of the Sangha is to create a safe place where people can get a taste of the peace, joy, and community that come with practice.

THICH NHAT HANH

CONSUMING MINDFULLY
TOGETHER

Our community should be organized in such a
way that sane, healthy kinds of nutriments will be
provided—not only edible food, sense-impres-
sion food, and wholesome desire but also a healthy
collective consciousness. It's very important to seek
a community where people practice compassion and
understanding and that we create that kind of environment for our children.

THE OPPORTUNITY TO LIVE
OUR LIFE FULLY

In our store consciousness is a wonderful seed called mindfulness, the capacity to be aware of what is happening in the present moment. That seed may be weak because we seldom water it. Generally, we don't go about our lives in a mindful way. We don't eat mindfully. We don't walk mindfully. We don't look at or speak to people mindfully. We live in forgetfulness. But we always have the opportunity to live our life fully. When we drink water, we can be aware that we're drinking water. When we walk, we can be aware that we're walking. Mindfulness is available to us at every moment.

I HAVE ARRIVED

We all have the tendency to struggle in our bodies and our minds. We believe that happiness is possible only in the future. That is why the practice "I have arrived" is very important. The realization that we have already arrived, that we don't have to travel any further, that we're already here, can give us peace and joy. The conditions for our happiness are already sufficient. We only need to allow ourselves to be in the present moment, and we will be able to touch them.

THE MIRACLE IS TO WALK
ON EARTH

Our true home is the present moment. To live in the
present moment is a miracle. The miracle isn't to walk
on water. The miracle is to walk on the green earth
in the present moment, to appreciate the peace and
beauty that are available now.

THICH NHAT HANH

TODAY'S DAY

Life is found only in the present moment. I think we should have a holiday to celebrate this fact. We have holidays for so many important occasions—Christmas, New Year's Day, Mother's Day, Father's Day, and even Earth Day. Why not celebrate a day when we can live happily in the present moment all day long? I would like to declare today "Today's Day," a day dedicated to touching the earth, touching the sky, touching the trees, and touching the peace that is available in the present moment.

HAS THE BEST MOMENT OF
YOUR LIFE ARRIVED YET?

We must stop destroying our body and soul for happiness in the future. We have to learn to live happily in the present moment, to touch the peace and joy that are available now. If someone were to ask us, "Has the best moment of your life arrived yet?" we may say that it will come very soon. But if we continue to live in the same way, it may never arrive. We have to transform this moment into the most wonderful moment, and we can do that by stopping—stopping running to the future, stopping worrying about the past. You are a free person; you are alive. Breathing in and out consciously helps you become your best—calm, fresh, solid, clear, and free, able to enjoy the present moment as the best moment of your life.

NO NEED FOR
IMPROVEMENT

We don't need to criticize ourselves or others for moments of forgetfulness. We don't even need to try to improve ourselves. All we need is to be in the moment, for the next one will be quite different. The present moment has all that we need.

PRACTICE IS NOT
HARD LABOR

We tend to think that if we work hard now, we'll be wealthier later. But it's not wise to work hard today to be happy tomorrow. We practice steadily and diligently but joyfully and happily at every moment. Practicing shouldn't be hard labor.

THE THEN WHICH
NEVER COMES

Many of us think that only once we have this or that,
only once the situation changes, only then can we
be happy. We don't recognize our happiness in the
now, and we seek it in the then. We have the idea that
happiness lies in some future moment. We say to one
another, "We have to wait, my beloved, and then..."
And while we busy ourselves trying to bring about that
then, we abandon our loved ones in the now. We sacri-
fice the now, which is so precious, for the then which
never comes.

YOU ALREADY ARE WHAT
YOU WANT TO BE

When we work too hard at anything, whether it's business or enlightenment, then we can't see the wonders of life inside and around us. You already are what you want to be. There is nothing to attain. Stop. Don't do anything. It may look like we aren't going anywhere, but in fact we're deeply in the present moment.

TRUE PRACTICE

When your practice is "true practice," it will bring
joy, peace, and stability to yourself and to the people
around you. To me, the practice should be pleasant. True practice can bring life to us right away. As
you practice mindful breathing, you become alive;
you become real. This happens not only when you
sit or walk but when you are making breakfast for
your beloved. If you know how to breathe in and out
mindfully while making breakfast with a smile, you
will cultivate freedom—from thinking about the past
or worrying about the future—aliveness, joy, and
compassion. While making breakfast, you can make
joy, peace, and compassion real. That is true practice,
and its effect can be seen right away.

ENJOYING SILENCE

Silence is something that comes from your heart, not from outside. Silence doesn't mean not talking and not doing things, but that you are not disturbed inside; there is no talking inside. If you are truly silent, then no matter where you find yourself you can enjoy the silence. There are moments when you think you're silent and all around is silent, but talking is going on inside your head. That's not silence. The practice is how to find silence in all the activities you do.

THICH NHAT HANH

ALL WE HAVE TO DO

Often we put an object in front of ourselves to chase after. That object may be nirvana or God, or it may be material wealth. We get tired running after this object, but all we have to do is stop. When we stop, we can have happiness. Our true nature is no different than the true nature of the great beings.

THE PRACTICE OF ARRIVAL

The place of arrival isn't somewhere else. The place of arrival is every minute, every second.

Life can be found in a step and in the space between steps. If we expect to see life outside each step and the space between steps, we don't have life. The great majority of people are running, and that is why the practice of arrival is so important. It's a drastic kind of medicine to heal us and our society because we carry, in each of us, the whole of society. The whole of society is running, and therefore we are running. Awakening can bring the desire to resist, to stop.

THICH NHAT HANH

BE TRULY ALIVE

Most of our thinking in our daily lives carries us away from the present moment. We get lost in the past and the future. This kind of thinking prevents us from being truly alive. In this context we can say: "I think, therefore I am not there." But right thinking helps us investigate the nature of things and understand the present moment.

SET OUR THINKING RIGHT

What is right thinking? It's the kind of thinking that helps you to understand more deeply, to be loving, to be compassionate, to be free. Right thinking reflects our deep understanding of reality. Right thinking reflects a situation as it is, free from wrong perceptions. It is possible to train ourselves to set our thinking right.

A GOOD WORK OF ART

When a painter creates a piece of art, they always sign their name. In your daily life you think, speak, and act. Your thoughts are your creation, and they always bear your name. If your thinking is right thinking, it's a good work of art.

YOUR LEGACY

If you think a thought of understanding and compassion, that is your creation, your legacy. Looking into your thinking, whether it's right or wrong, we see your signature. This is why, in our daily life, we must be careful to think thoughts that exhibit right thinking. You have an opportunity for right thinking at every moment of your life.

THICH NHAT HANH

NOTHING IS LOST

Suppose yesterday you generated an angry thought. That thought came from you; it's your continuation. But suppose today, after sitting and breathing, you realize that yesterday's angry thought wasn't right thinking. You're now determined to generate thoughts that are full of compassion, understanding, and forgiveness. As soon as you generate a wholesome thought, it will pursue the angry thought from yesterday and transform it. The Buddha teaches that because nothing is lost, you can repair the past.

Your angry thought from yesterday is your continuation. You don't want your continuation to be angry; you want it to be beautiful. You're capable of generating a beautiful thought today, and this has the capacity of catching the other thought and neutralizing it. This beautiful thought is also your continuation.

FREE FROM THE ROPES
THAT BIND US

If we continue to be imprisoned by the habit energies of the past, we will never liberate ourselves. We also won't liberate the thousands of generations of ancestors and descendants in us. But if we use the time while we're washing up, cleaning the vegetables, driving the car, or working in the garden to truly look at ourselves and each other, we see our true nature. In this way, we can gradually undo the ropes that bind us. Our fear, sorrow, and complexes are all born from our discriminating ideas of coming and going, self and other. Looking deeply like this in daily life is the true work of the practice, the cream of Buddhist teaching.

WE HAVE TO
TAKE THEM ALL

Habit energies are our only true belongings, the only heritage we'll continue to own when we die. Everything else—our loved ones, our home, our college degrees— we have to leave behind. All we take with us are our habit energies, and we can't choose only to take the ones we like; we have to take them all.

YOU ARE A MIRACLE

Dear friends, you are nothing less than a miracle. There may be times when you feel that you are worthless. But the fact that you're here—alive and capable of breathing in and out—is ample proof that you are a miracle. One string bean contains the whole cosmos in it: sunshine, rain, the whole earth, time, space, and consciousness. You also contain the whole cosmos.

THICH NHAT HANH

ETERNITY IN THE
PRESENT MOMENT

Eternity can be touched in this present moment, and the cosmos can be seen in the palm of our hand. But we need some mindfulness and concentration to do this. When you practice mindful walking or stretching, you can touch eternity with every movement. If you're truly mindful, if you're truly concentrated, if you can release the notion of self, you're no longer this tiny body. You're the whole cosmos. Your tiny body contains the whole cosmos in it. All the generations of the past and the future are there in your tiny body, and if you have that insight, it's easy to touch eternity in the present moment.

YOUR BODY IS NOT
YOURS ALONE

In the West, people have the impression that their body belongs to them, that they can do anything they want to their body. But according to the teaching of interbeing, your body is not yours alone. Your body belongs to your ancestors, your parents, and future generations, and it also belongs to society and all other living beings. All of them have come together to bring about the presence of this body.

WE ARE WHAT WE
CONSUME

Keeping your body healthy is an expression of gratitude to the whole cosmos—the trees, the clouds,
everything. If you're healthy, physically and mentally,
all of us will benefit. We are what we consume and
metabolize. Unless we consume mindfully, we may
destroy our body and our consciousness. Consuming
unmindfully, we express a lack of gratitude to our
ancestors, parents, and future generations.

THE HISTORY OF LIFE

When you remember to breathe in and out mindfully, your mind comes back to your body and back to the present moment. In the present moment, the first thing you encounter is your body. Getting in touch with your body, you see the history of life—you see your parents and your ancestors in you, not only human ancestors but also animal, plant, and mineral ancestors. You also see Mother Earth, Father Sun, and your spiritual ancestors in you. They are all alive and fully present in every cell of your body.

A CONTINUOUSLY
FLOWING STREAM

Looking into your body, you will discover that you aren't a separate self, cut off from everything else, but a continuously flowing stream—the stream of life itself.

LIBERATING ANCESTORS
AND FUTURE GENERATIONS

We have to live in a way that liberates the ancestors and future generations who are inside of us. Joy, peace, freedom, and harmony aren't individual matters. If we don't liberate our ancestors, we'll be in bondage all our lives, and we'll transmit that to our children and grandchildren. Now is the time to do it. Liberating them means liberating ourselves. As long as our ancestors in us are still suffering, we cannot really be happy. If we take one step mindfully, freely, happily touching the earth, we do it for all previous and future generations. They all arrive with us at the same moment, and all of us find peace at the same time.

THAT GREAT HEART
OUTSIDE OUR BODY

We know that if our heart stops beating, the flow of our life will stop, and so we cherish our heart very much. Yet we don't often take the time to notice that other things, outside our body, are also essential for our survival. Look at the immense light we call the sun. If it stops shining, the flow of our life will also stop. And so the sun is our second heart, our heart outside of our body. This immense "heart" gives all life on Earth the warmth necessary for existence. All of us—people, animals, and plants—"consume" the sun, directly and indirectly. We cannot begin to describe all the effects of the sun, that great heart outside our body.

SEE THE UNIVERSE
IN A PIECE OF BREAD

The food we eat is a gift from the earth. When you take a bite of bread or a sip of tea, do it with awareness. Your mind shouldn't be somewhere else, like thinking about your job or planning for the future. Looking deeply into the bread, see the golden wheat fields and the beautiful countryside around them; see the labor of the farmer, the miller, and the baker. The bread doesn't come from nothing. It comes from the grains, the rain, the sun, the soil, and the hard work of many people. The whole universe has brought this piece of bread to you. When you stop thinking and bring your mind home to the present moment, you can look deeply into the piece of bread and see this.

THICH NHAT HANH

DRINKING, NOT THINKING

When I drink tea with my full awareness, this is
mindful drinking. If I establish myself in the here and
now, my tea also becomes fully present. It is possible
to drink our tea and eat our breakfast mindfully. You
might ask: "I have so many things to take care of and
think about, how can I afford the time to drink my tea
mindfully?" But if you're lost in your thinking while
you drink your tea, it isn't true tea drinking. You aren't
real, and the tea isn't real. This is why nonthinking is a
very important practice.

HEALING WITH THE EARTH

We have so many reasons to be happy. The earth is
filled with love and patience for us. Whenever she sees
us suffering, she will protect us. With the earth as a
refuge, we need not be afraid of anything, even dying.
Walking mindfully on the earth, we're nourished by
the trees, the bushes, the flowers, and the sunshine.
We're children of the earth. We rely on the earth, and
the earth relies on us. Whether the earth is beautiful,
fresh, and green or arid and parched depends on our
way of walking. Please touch the earth in mindfulness,
with joy and concentration. The earth will heal you,
and you will heal the earth.

THE EARTH IS RIGHT HERE

The earth has all the virtues we seek, including strength, stability, patience, and compassion. She embraces everyone. We don't need blind faith to see this. We don't need to address our prayers or express our gratitude to a remote deity. The earth is right here; we can address our prayers directly to her. She supports us in very concrete and tangible ways. No one can deny that the water that sustains us, the air we breathe, and the food that nourishes us are gifts of the earth.

CONNECTING WITH
THE EARTH

When we recognize the virtues and talents of the earth, we feel connected to her, and love is born in our hearts. We want to be connected. That is the meaning of love: to be at one. When you love someone, you want to take care of that person as you would take care of yourself. When we love like this, it's reciprocal. We will do anything for the benefit of the earth. We can trust that, in turn, she will do everything in her power for our well-being.

WE ARE ALREADY HOME

To take refuge in the earth is to come back to our true home. There are those of us who live in very comfortable houses. You may have a roof over your head, a comfortable bed to sleep in, and sufficient food to eat, and yet you still don't feel at home. All of us are looking for our true home, the place where we feel safe and sheltered. If we practice mindful breathing to get in touch with the earth, then we'll know we're already home.

CITIZENS OF THE EARTH, UNITE!

Every one of us, regardless of nationality or religious faith, can experience admiration and love when we see the beauty of the earth. This feeling of love and admiration has the power to unite the citizens of the earth and remove all separation and discrimination.

THICH NHAT HANH

THRIVING TOGETHER

Caring about the environment isn't an obligation; it's a matter of personal and collective happiness and survival. We will survive and thrive together with Mother Earth, or we will not survive at all.

PARADISE ON EARTH

A few decades ago, when the astronauts of Apollo went into outer space and looked back at the planet Earth, they saw a very beautiful planet. They took a picture and sent it back to us, and it was the first time we saw our planet from a distance. In our solar system, we have not found a place like planet Earth. Everywhere else, the environment is hostile to human life. Only on planet Earth is life possible. Earth is a bastion of life. It's really a paradise.

ABANDONING OUR VIEWS

In Buddhism, knowledge is regarded as an obstacle to understanding, like a block of ice that obstructs water from flowing. It's said that if we take one thing to be the truth and cling to it, then even if truth itself knocks at our door, we won't open it. For things to reveal themselves to us, we need to be ready to abandon our views about them.

REALITY BEYOND
CONCEPTS

Without a mind free from preconceived ideas, we
cannot penetrate reality. Scientists are coming to
realize that they cannot use ordinary language to
describe non-conceptual insights. Scientific language is
beginning to have the symbolic nature of poetry. Today
such words as "charm" and "color" are being used to
describe properties of particles that have no conceptual
counterpart in the "macro-realm." Someday reality
will reveal itself beyond all conceptualizations and
measurements.

THE ONE CONTAINS
THE ALL

The present moment contains past and future. The one contains the all. Time contains space. When we're in contact with the present moment, we're in contact with all time, including the past and future. Since time also contains space, the present moment also contains this place and all other places. Standing on the earth's surface, dwelling in the present moment, the ground under our feet is boundless. Standing in Paris, we see that we're standing on the whole of Europe. And if we remain firmly and solidly in the present moment, we see that we're also standing on Asia, the Americas, Africa, and the whole earth. In the present moment, we can touch the whole world and the whole universe.

A TOPIC FOR MEDITATION

Someday, if you need a topic for meditation, choose
one that you find very interesting so it will command
your attention. It can be the sun, a caterpillar, a
dewdrop, time, or your face before you were born.
Every phenomenon—concrete or abstract, physical,
physiological, psychological, or metaphysical—can
be the subject of your meditation. After you choose a
topic, plant it in the depths of your spiritual life. An
egg needs to be incubated by its mother hen to become
a baby chick. In the same way, the topic you sow must
be nurtured.

THICH NHAT HANH

ANY SUBJECT CAN BRING
ABOUT AWAKENING

Any subject can bring about awakening if it's sown deeply into the ground of your being. But if it's only entrusted to your intellect, it's unlikely to bear fruit.

TOUCHING NIRVANA

We come to the practice of meditation seeking relief from our suffering. Meditation can teach us how to transform our suffering and obtain basic relief. But the deepest kind of relief is the realization of nirvana. There are two dimensions to life, and we should be able to touch both. One is like a wave, and we call it the historical dimension. The other is like the water, and we call it the ultimate dimension, or nirvana. We usually touch just the wave, but when we discover how to touch the water, we receive the highest fruit that meditation can offer.

SINCE THE VERY
NON-BEGINNING

Nirvana means extinction—the extinction of all notions and concepts, including the concepts of birth, death, being, nonbeing, coming, and going. Nirvana is the ultimate dimension of life, a state of coolness, peace, and joy. It is not a state to be attained after you die. You can touch nirvana right now by breathing, walking, and drinking your tea in mindfulness. You have been "nirvanized" since the very non-beginning. Everything and everyone is dwelling in nirvana.

NIRVANA IS NONTHINKING

Another word for nirvana is nonthinking. You don't
need to think. Instead, you taste this; you feel that.
Nirvana is total freedom. It's equal to God with a
capital G. In Christianity there is the expression
"resting in God." This means you release all notions,
and you rest in freedom, in solidity, in the huge heart
of compassion.

TASTE NIRVANA
FOR YOURSELF

You have to taste nirvana for yourself. If someone asks you, "What does a kiwi taste like?" you would struggle to answer.

"Like an orange?"

"No."

"Is it like a mango?"

"No."

But if you put a piece of kiwi in their mouth, they know the nature of kiwi right away. There is no word to describe the kiwi; we just taste it. Nirvana is the same. There is no need to use all this vocabulary to describe nirvana; you have to taste it for yourself.

NONFEAR IS THE
GROUND OF PEACE

The purpose of Zen is to look deeply to realize our true nature: no birth and no death, no coming and no going, no being and no nonbeing, no sameness and no otherness. When we're capable of removing all these notions, we touch our true nature, and we touch nonfear. Nonfear is the ground of peace. It's the ground of true happiness.

THICH NHAT HANH

On the surface of the sea of phenomena, we see many waves glistening, but each wave's formation and destruction depends on every other wave. The memories of each of us aren't just our own personal treasures. They are living realities that are related to all other living realities. They undergo ceaseless trans-formation, as do our bodies. Each thing is reality, but reality isn't subject to ideas of "one" or "many."

VISUALIZING THE WORLD
100 YEARS FROM NOW

When we dwell in the historical dimension, we're tossed about by many waves. Perhaps we have a difficult time at work. Or we have to wait too long in line at the supermarket. Or we have an unpleasant conversation with our friend. We feel tired, a little depressed, or angry. This is because we're caught in the present situation. But if we close our eyes and visualize the world 100 years from now, we'll see that these problems aren't important. Embracing just 100 years, we see things very differently. Imagine how drastic a change is brought about by touching the ultimate dimension!

THE MIND IS THERE,
THE MOUNTAIN IS THERE

Our minds create everything. The majestic mountain-top, brilliant with snow, is you yourself when you contemplate it. Its existence depends on your awareness. When you close your eyes, if your mind is present, the mountain is there.

HOW TO SEE BETTER

Sitting in meditation, with several sense-windows closed, you feel the presence of the whole universe. Why? Because the mind is there. If your eyes are closed, you can see better.

THICH NHAT HANH

THE ONE IN THE MANY,
THE MANY IN THE ONE

When we look at a chair, we see the wood, but we
fail to see the tree, the forest, the carpenter, or our
own mind. When we meditate on it, we can see the
entire universe—all its interwoven and interdepen-
dent relations—in the chair. The presence of the wood
reveals the presence of the tree. The presence of the
leaf reveals the presence of the sun. The presence of
the apple blossom reveals the presence of the apple.
Meditators can see the one in the many and the many
in the one.

THE CHAIR HAS NO
BEGINNING AND NO END

Every time we use the word "chair," or the concept "chair" forms in our mind, reality is severed in half. There is "chair," and there is everything that is "not chair." This kind of separation is both violent and absurd. The sword of conceptualization functions this way because we don't realize that the chair is made entirely of non-chair elements. Since all non-chair elements are present in the chair, how can we separate them? An awakened individual looking at the chair clearly sees the non-chair elements. They realize that the chair has no boundaries, no beginning, and no end.

THE FREEDOM OF A LEAF

When we step on a leaf during walking meditation, our
mindfulness helps us see deeply into the nature of the
leaf. It seems to be dying, disintegrating into the earth.
In fact, this is just an appearance. If we look deeply
into the nature of the leaf, we can see that the leaf is
one with the tree. There is a moment when the leaf
pretends to be born and a moment when it pretends to
die. These are just appearances. Deep in its nature, the
leaf is free from birth and death. It's a manifestation.

ALL IS IN THE WORD
"KNOW"

Most people view themselves as waves and forget that they are also water. They are used to living in the historical dimension of birth and death, and they forget about no birth and no death. But a wave also lives the life of water, and we also live the life of no birth and no death. We only need to know that we're living the life of no birth and no death. All is in the word "know." To know is to realize. Realization is mindfulness. All the work of meditation is aimed at realizing only one thing: birth and death can never touch us in any way whatsoever.

YOU CAN'T DESTROY
A HUMAN BEING

Many people believe that there's nothing left after the disintegration of the body. But our thoughts, our speech, and our actions are the energies we produce, and they will continue for a long time. You can't destroy a human being. You can't reduce them to nonbeing. Looking deeply like that into our true nature, into the nature of other people around you, you'll have the kind of insight that will liberate you from sorrow, fear, and anger.

LIBERATION, EVERY DAY

Every day is an opportunity for us to practice liberation—liberating our ancestors and our descendants within us. With meditation, we can relive the moments of our life that have been full of fear and suffering, practice mindful breathing, and breathe for all our ancestors and all our descendants. When I'm breathing, I'm not breathing for one mother and one child but for many mothers and many children. Breathing like that for ten minutes can bring liberation if we practice properly.

REPAIRING THE PAST

We think that the past is gone and the future is not yet here. But if we look deeply, we see that reality is more than that. The past exists in the guise of the present because the present is made from the past. If we establish ourselves firmly in the present, touching the present moment deeply, we also touch the past and have the power to repair it. That is a wonderful teaching and practice. We don't have to bear our wounds forever.

LONG LIVE IMPERMANENCE

Using our intelligence and insight, we recognize how crucial impermanence is to life. Impermanence allows us to transform and move in a better direction. Without impermanence, dictatorships or illnesses would last forever. Impermanence isn't a pessimistic note in the music of reality; in fact, it's vital for there to be life at all. Instead of complaining about impermanence, we should say, "Long live impermanence."

THE INSIGHT OF
IMPERMANENCE

The insight of impermanence isn't just an intellectual
understanding. There is a big difference between the
idea of impermanence and the insight of impermanence. The teaching of impermanence is offered only
so that we can realize the insight of impermanence. To
get the insight, we must make use of this teaching in
an intelligent way. We must take care not to get caught
in dogma, in a conceptual understanding of impermanence, nonself, and nirvana. We have to transform what
we learn into real insight and keep this insight alive in
our daily life.

THE INSIGHT CONSUMES
THE NOTION

The notion of impermanence may be an instrument to bring about the insight of impermanence. In the same way, a match isn't a flame, but it can bring about a flame. When you have the flame, it will consume the match. What you need is the flame, not the match. What you need to be liberated is the insight of impermanence, not the notion of impermanence. But at first, the notion of impermanence can help generate the insight of impermanence. When the insight of impermanence is there, it burns up the notion of impermanence.

ILLUMINATE YOUR
DAILY LIFE

We cannot liberate ourselves with a mere notion. We can talk about impermanence all we want, but without real insight, there will be no change in our lives. If you can practice looking deeply to transform your notions of impermanence and nonself into the flame of real insight, that insight will illuminate your daily life, moment to moment. You will know what to do and what not to do to bring well-being and happiness to yourself and others.

YOUR MOTHER'S HAND

Remember when you were small, had a fever, and felt so alone, but your mother suddenly appeared like an angel? She touched your forehead with her hand, full of love and concern, and you felt wonderful. Even if your mother is no longer alive, if you know how to touch her, she will be born again within you. This is your hand, but it's also your mother's hand; your hand is a continuation of her hand. If you want to feel your mother's hand touch your forehead, go ahead. Your mother is alive within you.

THICH NHAT HANH

PRACTICING WITH OUR PARENTS

Many of us have suffered because of our parents. Some of us say, "I don't want to have anything to do with my parents." This isn't possible because we are the continuation of our parents; we are our parents. There is no way to escape this. The only way is to have some reconciliation with ourselves and with our internal parents.

RECOGNIZING THE
TRANSMISSION

We have been victims of negative behavior and negative
seeds. But by practicing deeply, we realize that the
other person may also have been the victim of a particular seed's transmission. They never met a teacher and
a Sangha, and the seed was not transformed. Later,
it was transmitted to us. When you see your parents
as victims of transmission, your anger will vanish.
Looking deeply like this to generate understanding and
freedom from your anger is very important.

INTERGENERATIONAL
HEALING

We can achieve transformation not only for ourselves, but for our fathers, our mothers, and our ancestors. When I practice breathing in and calming and breathing out and smiling, I'm liberating my father, my mother, and my ancestors. I'm also liberating my children and their children. Every time I take a peaceful, happy step, I take it for all my ancestors. This practice helps us to transform and heal. We do it for everyone at the same time. Only through such practice is true reconciliation possible.

WE CANNOT BE BY OURSELVES ALONE

The flower is full of everything in the cosmos, except one thing: a separate self, a separate existence. This is the insight of the Buddha. This is important. With meditation, mindfulness, and concentration, we can look deeply into the flower and discover the nature of emptiness. The flower is empty of what? It's empty of a separate existence, but at the same time, it's totally full of the cosmos. This is the case of the flower, the table, the house, and the river. We cannot be by ourselves alone. We have to inter-be with everyone else, with everything else.

THICH NHAT HANH

EVERY KIND OF FLOWER
IS BEAUTIFUL

The wisdom of interbeing helps us touch the wisdom of nondiscrimination. It sets us free. With the wisdom of interbeing, there is no more discrimination, no more hatred. We no longer wish to belong to just one geographical area or cultural identity. Looking into ourselves, we can see a multitude of ethnic sources, a multitude of cultural sources, and we can see the presence of the whole cosmos. We may manifest as a lotus flower, a magnolia flower, or an orange flower, but every kind of flower is beautiful, whatever its shape and color.

ELEMENTS OF TRUE LOVE

We suffer because our hearts are too small; they tend to exclude and eliminate. Loving kindness, compassion, joy, and equanimity are the real elements of true love. They have the capacity to receive, embrace, and transform everything.

MAKE YOUR HEART
LIKE THE RIVER

If you stir a handful of salt into a bowl of water, the water becomes too salty to drink. If you pour that water into a river, the river is too large to be affected. If your heart is like the river, you won't suffer because of small problems.

TOUCHING NONSELF

We should not get caught up in the idea of nonself.
Nonself doesn't mean not existing; it means that there
are no separate entities. When you get in touch with
yourself, you get in touch with your father, your child,
the sunshine, and the clouds. Everything in the cosmos
has come together for you to manifest.

YOU ARE HERE

You are made of non-you elements, which doesn't mean that you aren't here. The self that we speak of as a separate entity is just a notion, a concept. With the practice of looking deeply, we can make that concept evaporate, and then we are free.

OUR TRUE PERSON

Our true person can't be found by means of our intellect, our reasoning. On this pile of red flesh, there's a true person. If you haven't seen this person, look carefully. Live mindfully. Our true person is our own miraculous buddha, present in our wonderful relationship with all things.

WE ARE MORE THAN THAT

Our buddha isn't our five skandhas, the five things that make up a human being: form, feelings, perceptions, mental formations, and consciousness. These aren't our true person. We are the clouds, the sky, all our ancestors and descendants. Our true person is a wonder. And when we can see this, we are well. We still have our ups and downs, but we don't identify ourselves with them; we know we're more than that. Our great success as practitioners is to realize our true person.

DON'T LOOK FOR FRESH
WATER IN DRY BONES

Insight can't be found in sutras, commentaries, or Dharma talks. Liberation and awakened understanding can't be found by devoting ourselves to the study of the Buddhist scriptures. This is like hoping to find fresh water in dry bones. Returning to the present moment, using our clear mind that exists right here and now, we can be in touch with liberation and enlightenment. We can be in touch with the Buddha and all his disciples as living realities right in this moment.

THICH NHAT HANH

A MUSTARD SEED
IN YOUR HEART

In the Gospel of Matthew, Jesus says, "Just take care of today. Don't worry about tomorrow. Tomorrow will take care of itself." This is the same teaching found in Buddhism: live in the here and now and don't worry too much about the future. And the Kingdom of God is a mustard seed in your heart. If we know how to plant that seed in the soil of our life, it will become a tree where many birds can take refuge.

THE PATH IS HERE

The Path isn't a dream. It isn't a wish. The Path is concrete practice. And it will save our life. It will save our children. If we're on the Path, then from within us a stream of compassion and loving kindness arises and our suffering eases. We don't have to go anywhere. The solution doesn't lie in some other place.

THICH NHAT HANH

RESTING WITH GOD

On my last trip to the United States, a friend requested that I write a calligraphy for him of the phrase "Resting with God." I wrote it for him because it embodies the realization that God is here; he isn't an old man with a beard sitting high above us. He is our true nature, our suchness, just as the water is the suchness of the wave. And if the wave knows how to take refuge in the water, if it knows to believe in the water, then the wave loses all its fears, sadness, and jealousy. If we take refuge in our true nature, then we aren't afraid anymore of gaining, losing, having, not having, living, dying, being, and nonbeing.

THERE IS NO OBSTACLE

If we want to be the Buddha sitting on the lotus, nobody will stop us. There's no obstacle. We have so many opportunities in our daily life to be the Buddha sitting on the lotus, and yet we don't do it. The house of the Buddha has so much room, and yet we don't live in it. We just sleep outside.

NONATTAINMENT

Everywhere people talk about the Path. If there's
practice, then there's attainment. Don't be mistaken.
Even if you attain the Path, or the fruit of the practice,
that's only the karma of birth and death. Nonattain-
ment means that there's nothing we don't have now
that we'll have in the future.

SPIRITUALITY IS A
PRACTICE

Spirituality isn't just belief in a teaching; it's a practice. And the practice always brings relief, communication, and transformation. Everyone needs a spiritual dimension in their life. Without a spiritual dimension in our life, we cannot deal with our difficulties.

We learn how to put the Dharma into practice. With that kind of practice, we can deal with whatever we encounter in our daily life.

A FESTIVAL OF LIFE

Every moment of your daily life can be a moment of
celebrating life; it depends on you. You have the talent
to organize things so that life becomes a festival.

A RIVER OF UNDERSTANDING

When we decide to live our lives with love and awakening, we enter a flowing river of understanding and compassion. That river has no beginning and no end. It contains our Sangha, our ancestors, and future generations. I invite all of us, together as one, to relax and be carried by this river, to let it take us where we want to go.

THE SUN OF AWARENESS

Where are you now, my good friend? Are you out in the field, in the forest, on the mountain, in a military camp, in a factory, at your desk, in a hospital, in prison? Regardless of where you are, let us breathe in and out together and allow the sun of aware-ness to enter. Let us begin with this breath and this awareness. Whether life is an illusion, a dream, or a wondrous reality depends on our insight and our mindfulness. Awakening is a miracle. The darkness in a totally dark room will disappear the moment the light is switched on. In the same way, the second the sun of awareness begins to shine, life will reveal itself as a miraculous reality.

MINDFUL CLOSING

One day, my teacher told me to go do something for him. I loved him so much that I was very eager to do it, so I closed the door after me unmindfully. He called me back.

"My child."

"Yes?"

"Go out again and close the door mindfully this time."

I understood. He never had to tell me again. I knew how to close the door mindfully from that moment on.

THICH NHAT HANH

Monastics and visitors practice the art of mindful living in the tradition of Thich Nhat Hanh at our mindfulness practice centers around the world. To reach any of these communities, or for information about how individuals, couples, and families can join in a retreat, please contact:

PLUM VILLAGE
13 Martineau
33580 Dieulivol, France
plumvillage.org

MAGNOLIA GROVE MONASTERY
123 Towles Road
Batesville, MS 38606, USA
magnoliagrovemonastery.org

BLUE CLIFF MONASTERY
3 Mindfulness Road
Pine Bush, NY 12566, USA
bluecliffmonastery.org

DEER PARK MONASTERY
2499 Melru Lane
Escondido, CA 92026, USA
deerparkmonastery.org

EUROPEAN INSTITUTE OF
APPLIED BUDDHISM
Schaumburgweg 3
D-51545 Waldbröl, Germany
eiab.eu

THAILAND PLUM VILLAGE
Pong Ta Long, Pak Chong
District
Nakhon Ratchasima
30130 Thailand
thaiplumvillage.org

ASIAN INSTITUTE OF APPLIED
BUDDHISM
Ngong Ping
Lantau Island, Hong Kong
pvfhk.org

LE MONASTÈRE DE A MAISON
DE L'INSPIR
8 Rue des Fans
77510 Villeneuve-sur-Bellot,
France
maisondelinspir.org

HEALING SPRING MONASTERY
2 Rue Pascal Jardin
77510 Verdelot, France
healingspringmonastery.org

STREAM ENTERING MONASTERY
221 Marias Lane
Beaufort, Victoria 3373,
Australia
nhapluu.org

The Mindfulness Bell, a journal of the art of mindful living in the tradition of Thich Nhat Hanh, is published three times a year by our community. To subscribe or to see the world-wide directory of Sanghas (local mindfulness groups), visit mindfulnessbell.org.

planting seeds of Compassion

The Thich Nhat Hanh Foundation works to continue the mindful teachings and practice of Zen Master Thich Nhat Hanh, in order to foster peace and transform suffering in all people, animals, plants, and our planet. Through donations to the Foundation, thousands of generous supporters ensure the continuation of Plum Village practice centers and monastics around the world, bring transformative practices to those who otherwise would not be able to access them, support local mindfulness initiatives, and bring humanitarian relief to communities in crisis in Vietnam.

By becoming a supporter, you join many others who want to learn and share these life-changing practices of mindfulness, loving speech, deep listening, and compassion for oneself, each other, and the planet.

For more information on how you can help support mindfulness around the world, or to subscribe to the Foundation's monthly newsletter with teachings, news, and global retreats, visit tnhf.org.

FURTHER RESOURCES

For information about our international community,
visit: plumvillage.org

To find an online sangha, visit: plumline.org

For more practices and resources, download the
Plum Village app: plumvillage.app